The Jezebel Effect - Ancient Manipulations Modern Lessons

Joshua Rhoades

Published by Joshua Paul Rhoades, 2024.

While every precaution has been taken in the preparation of this book, the publisher assumes no responsibility for errors or omissions, or for damages resulting from the use of the information contained herein.

THE JEZEBEL EFFECT - ANCIENT MANIPULATIONS MODERN LESSONS

First edition. August 31, 2024.

Copyright © 2024 Joshua Rhoades.

ISBN: 979-8224514588

Written by Joshua Rhoades.

Also by Joshua Rhoades

Courage Under Fire: David's Stand On The Battlefield
Jonah's Journey: Voices Of Redemption And Lessons In Obedience
The Furnace Of Faith: 12 Principles From The Heat Of Faith
Whispers of Hope: Inspiring Stories of Men's Prayers In Scripture
Frontier Legends: The Oregon Dream
Elijah: A Beacon Of Boldness
HOOK, LINE & SAVIOUR - Faith Reflections from Fishing
Driven By Faith: Motor Racing Inspired Christian Life
30 Day Devotional - Bold and Strong- Coffee Devotions for a
Courageous Christian Walk
Authentic Christianity: The Heart of Old Time Religion
Consider The Ant - God's Tiny Preachers
Flee Fornication: The Plea For Purity
Renewed Hope- How to Find Encouragement in God
Sounding The Call - The Voice of Conviction
The Altar - Where Heaven Meets Earth
The Bible's Battlefields- Timeless Lessons from Ancient Wars
The Sacred Art of Silence - How Silence Speaks in Scripture
Under Fire- The Sanctity of the Traditional Biblical Home
Who Is on the Lord's Side? A Call to Righteousness
What Is Truth? - From Skepticism to Submission
First and Goal- Faith and Football Fundamentals
From Dugout to Devotion- Spiritual Lessons from Baseball
Par for the Course- Faith and Fairways
The Believer's Pace- Tools for Running Life's Marathon

The Immutable Fortress- Security in God's Unchanging Nature
Biblical Bravery
The Jezebel Effect - Ancient Manipulations Modern Lessons

Introduction
Chapter 1 - Sinful
Chapter 2 – Slaughter
Chapter 3 – Slaying
Chapter 4 -Sword
Chapter 5 – Sent
Chapter 6 – Sad
Chapter 7 – Scheming
Chapter 8 – Subordinates
Chapter 9 – Stoned
Chapter 10 – Seizing
Chapter 11 – The Sentencing
Chapter 12 – Stirred
Chapter 13 – The Smiting
Chapter 14 – Shamed
Chapter 15 – Sorceries
Chapter 16 – Sight
Chapter 17 – Statement
Chapter 18 – Scorned
Chapter 19 – Seduce
Conclusion

Introduction

"The Jezebel Effect: Ancient Manipulations, Modern Lessons" delves into the timeless and chilling story of Jezebel, one of the most infamous figures in the Bible, as portrayed in the King James Version. Jezebel, the queen whose name has become synonymous with cunning, deceit, and ruthless ambition, left a mark on history that echoes far beyond the ancient world. Her story, rooted in the pages of 1 and 2 Kings, is not just a historical account of manipulation and power, but a powerful cautionary tale that offers critical insights into the nature of influence, control, and moral decay—lessons that are strikingly relevant in our modern world.

In this book, we explore the character of Jezebel, not just as a figure of ancient times, but as a representation of a pervasive spirit that continues to manifest in various forms today. Her methods of manipulation, her use of power to achieve personal gain, and her ultimate downfall serve as potent reminders of the dangers that arise when individuals or even entire societies stray from the principles of integrity, truth, and reverence for God. Jezebel's story is one of spiritual and moral corruption, but it is also a story of God's justice and the consequences of unchecked evil.

"The Jezebel Effect" seeks to unpack the layers of Jezebel's character and actions, drawing connections between her ancient tactics and the ways in which similar strategies of manipulation and control are employed in our contemporary world. Whether in personal relationships, corporate environments, or political arenas, the echoes of Jezebel's influence can be seen in how power is wielded, how truth is twisted, and how individuals and societies can be led astray by seductive promises of control and dominance. By examining the biblical account and applying its lessons to today's world, this book offers readers a deeper understanding of the spiritual and ethical implications of manipulation and deceit.

Through the lens of the King James Bible, we will explore the biblical narrative, dissecting the strategies Jezebel used to manipulate those around her, and drawing parallels to modern-day scenarios where similar tactics are at play. This exploration is not just an academic exercise, but a call to vigilance—urging readers to recognize and resist the Jezebel spirit in whatever form it appears. Whether it's in the subtle pressures of societal norms, the overt power plays in politics, or the personal struggles for control in relationships, "The Jezebel Effect" provides a framework for understanding these dynamics and offers practical wisdom on how to navigate and overcome them.

Ultimately, "The Jezebel Effect" is a book about the power of influence, the dangers of moral compromise, and the enduring relevance of biblical truth. By learning from the story of Jezebel, readers are equipped not only to recognize manipulation in its various forms but also to stand firm in their convictions, guided by the enduring principles of the Bible. This book invites readers to reflect on the lessons of the past, apply them to the present, and seek to build a future grounded in integrity, truth, and a steadfast commitment to God's righteous standards.

Chapter 1 - Sinful

I Kings 16:31 "And it came to pass, as if it had been a light thing for him to walk in the sins of Jeroboam the son of Nebat, that he took to wife Jezebel the daughter of Ethbaal king of the Zidonians, and went and served Baal, and worshipped him."

Jezebel, a character from the Bible, is widely known for her sinful and destructive behavior, particularly as described in 1 Kings 16:31. This verse explains how she influenced King Ahab to engage in sinful acts, leading him away from the worship of the true God and towards the worship of Baal, a false god. Jezebel, being the daughter of Ethbaal, king of the Zidonians, brought with her the practices of idol worship, and her influence over Ahab led to great sins in the kingdom of Israel. Her actions were not just personal failures; they had widespread consequences, leading an entire nation astray. Jezebel's behavior in this context can be seen as an example of how powerful leaders can use their influence to lead others into wrongdoing. In today's world, we can draw parallels to various scenarios where leaders, whether in politics, business, or other areas, use their power and influence to promote harmful or unethical behaviors. For instance, when leaders prioritize their own interests over the well-being of the people they serve, they can cause widespread harm, just as Jezebel did. This might be seen in the way some political leaders push for policies that benefit a select few while causing harm to the broader community. Similarly, in the corporate world, there are instances where business leaders engage in unethical practices, such as exploiting workers, harming the environment, or engaging in corrupt activities to maximize profits. These actions can have devastating effects on society, much like how Jezebel's actions led to spiritual and moral decay in Israel.

Moreover, Jezebel's story highlights the danger of idolatry and turning away from true values and principles. Today, this can be compared to how some individuals or societies place excessive value on wealth, power, and material success, often at the expense of ethical and moral values. This modern form of idolatry can lead to various negative outcomes, including social inequality, environmental degradation, and a loss of community and spiritual connection. Just as Jezebel's worship of Baal led the Israelites away from their faith, today's society can sometimes lose sight of important values in the pursuit of superficial or materialistic goals.

Jezebel's manipulation and control over Ahab also reflect how toxic relationships and influences can lead individuals to make poor decisions. In contemporary times, this might be seen in various forms of manipulation and control, whether in personal relationships, workplace dynamics, or broader social and political contexts. People may be pressured or influenced to act against their better judgment, leading to harmful consequences. For example, peer pressure can lead individuals, especially young people, to engage in risky or harmful behaviors. In the workplace, employees might feel compelled to go along with unethical practices to keep their jobs or gain favor with superiors. Politically, citizens might be swayed by charismatic leaders who promise quick fixes or appeal to their fears and prejudices, leading to divisive and harmful policies.

Additionally, Jezebel's story illustrates the importance of accountability and the consequences of unchecked power. Jezebel's actions went largely unchallenged by Ahab, leading to widespread corruption and idolatry. In today's world, this serves as a reminder of the need for checks and balances in all areas of life, from government and business to personal relationships. When individuals or institutions hold too much power without accountability, it can lead to abuse and corruption. This is why democratic systems emphasize the importance of checks and balances, transparency, and accountability to prevent the concentration of power and ensure that leaders act in the best interests of the people they serve.

Furthermore, Jezebel's influence on Ahab can be seen as a warning about the dangers of surrounding oneself with negative influences. Just as Ahab's association with Jezebel led him away from his faith and towards sinful behavior, individuals today can be negatively impacted by the company they keep. This highlights the importance of choosing friends, mentors, and advisors who uphold positive values and encourage ethical behavior. Surrounding oneself with positive influences can lead to personal growth and better decision-making, while negative influences can lead to destructive behavior and poor choices.

In conclusion, Jezebel's behavior as described in 1 Kings 16:31 provides a powerful example of the destructive potential of sinful and unethical behavior, especially when it comes from a position of influence. Her story is a timeless reminder of the importance of maintaining strong values, resisting negative influences, and ensuring accountability in all areas of life. By reflecting on Jezebel's actions and their consequences, we can better understand the importance of ethical leadership, the dangers of idolatry and materialism, and the need for positive influences and accountability in our own lives. Whether in ancient times or today, the lessons from Jezebel's story remain relevant and important for promoting a just, ethical, and compassionate society.

Chapter 2 – Slaughter

I Kings 18:4 "For it was so, when Jezebel cut off the prophets of the LORD, that Obadiah took an hundred prophets, and hid them by fifty in a cave, and fed them with bread and water."

Jezebel's behavior in the Bible, particularly as described in 1 Kings 18:4, is remembered for its cruelty and violence, especially towards the prophets of the Lord. In this verse, it is stated that Jezebel cut off the prophets of the Lord, which means she ordered their slaughter. This act of killing God's prophets shows her complete disregard for the worship of the true God and her determination to eliminate anyone who stood against her beliefs and authority. Jezebel's ruthless actions forced Obadiah, a servant of King Ahab who feared the Lord, to hide a hundred prophets in a cave and provide them with bread and water to save their lives. This historical act of persecution can be compared to modern instances where people face oppression and violence for their religious beliefs or for standing up against powerful authorities.

In today's world, similar behaviors can be observed in various forms of religious persecution. Many countries still face significant issues with religious intolerance, where individuals are harassed, imprisoned, or even killed for their faith. This is particularly evident in regions where there is a lack of religious freedom and where governments or dominant religious groups oppress minority faiths. Just as Jezebel used her power to silence the prophets, modern-day oppressors use their influence to suppress religious expression and eliminate dissenting voices. This results in a climate of fear and repression, where people are afraid to practice their faith openly or speak out against injustices.

Furthermore, Jezebel's actions can also be seen in the context of political persecution, where governments or leaders target and eliminate those who oppose them. In many parts of the world, political dissidents, activists, and journalists face threats, imprisonment, and violence for challenging corrupt regimes or authoritarian rulers. These modern instances of persecution are reminiscent of how Jezebel sought to consolidate her power by eliminating those who opposed her. The tactics used by oppressive regimes today, such as censorship, intimidation, and extrajudicial killings, mirror the brutal methods Jezebel employed to maintain her authority and suppress opposition.

Additionally, Jezebel's slaughter of the prophets highlights the dangers of unchecked power and the absence of accountability. When leaders hold absolute power without any checks and balances, they can act with impunity, leading to widespread abuse and violence. This is why democratic systems and institutions that promote transparency and accountability are essential for preventing such abuses of power. In contemporary society, efforts to ensure governmental accountability, protect human rights, and uphold the rule of law are crucial in preventing the kind of tyranny and violence exemplified by Jezebel's actions.

Moreover, the story of Jezebel's slaughter of the prophets underscores the importance of protecting and supporting those who are vulnerable to persecution. Just as Obadiah took great risks to hide and provide for the prophets, modern-day efforts to protect persecuted individuals and communities are vital. This includes providing asylum for refugees fleeing religious or political persecution, supporting human rights organizations, and advocating for policies that promote religious freedom and protect minority groups. The compassion and bravery shown by individuals and organizations that work to protect the persecuted are essential in countering the effects of oppressive actions similar to those carried out by Jezebel.

The parallels between Jezebel's actions and modern-day persecution also highlight the ongoing struggle for religious and political freedom. The need to stand up against tyranny and protect the rights of individuals to express their beliefs and opinions remains as relevant today as it was in Jezebel's time. Advocacy for religious tolerance, freedom of speech, and human rights continues to be a critical aspect of creating a just and equitable society. The story of Jezebel serves as a reminder of the consequences of allowing power to go unchecked and the importance of vigilance in protecting the freedoms that are essential to human dignity and social harmony.

Furthermore, Jezebel's willingness to commit such atrocities to maintain her power reflects a broader theme of how leaders can become corrupted by their desire for control. This is evident in contemporary examples of leaders who go to great lengths, including committing human rights abuses, to retain their positions of power. The use of violence, propaganda, and coercion to suppress opposition and maintain control is a tactic that has been employed by many authoritarian regimes throughout history and continues to be a significant issue in many parts of the world today.

In conclusion, Jezebel's behavior as described in 1 Kings 18:4, where she ordered the slaughter of the prophets of the Lord, is a stark example of the dangers of unchecked power, religious intolerance, and political persecution. Her actions forced individuals like Obadiah to take extraordinary measures to protect the innocent and uphold their faith. The parallels to modern-day instances of religious and political persecution, the importance of accountability and transparency, and the ongoing struggle for freedom and human rights highlight the enduring relevance of Jezebel's story. By reflecting on her actions and their consequences, we can better understand the critical importance of protecting religious and political freedoms, supporting those who are vulnerable to persecution, and ensuring that power is held accountable. The lessons from Jezebel's story serve as a timeless reminder of the need to promote justice, tolerance, and human dignity in our world today.

Chapter 3 – Slaying

I Kings 18:13 "Was it not told my lord what I did when Jezebel slew the prophets of the LORD, how I hid an hundred men of the LORD'S prophets by fifty in a cave, and fed them with bread and water?

In the Bible, Jezebel's behavior is depicted as particularly ruthless and violent, especially in 1 Kings 18:13, where it is recounted how she killed the prophets of the Lord. This verse highlights her extreme cruelty and her determination to eradicate those who worshipped and served God. Jezebel's actions were aimed at consolidating her power and promoting the worship of Baal, the false god she brought with her from her homeland. Her willingness to slay the prophets demonstrates a complete disregard for human life and a deep-seated hatred for those who opposed her beliefs. In today's world, we can draw parallels between Jezebel's behavior and the actions of certain leaders and regimes that use violence and oppression to maintain control and silence dissent.

In modern times, we see similar acts of brutality in countries where there is a lack of religious freedom and where governments or militant groups persecute religious minorities. Just as Jezebel sought to eliminate the prophets of the Lord, these contemporary oppressors target individuals and groups who practice different faiths or hold different beliefs. This persecution can take many forms, including imprisonment, torture, and even execution. For example, in some countries, people are imprisoned or killed for converting to a different religion or for practicing their faith openly. These actions create a climate of fear and force individuals to hide their beliefs, much like the prophets who had to go into hiding during Jezebel's reign.

Additionally, Jezebel's behavior can be compared to the actions of authoritarian regimes that seek to silence political opposition through violence and intimidation. In many parts of the world, political dissidents, journalists, and activists face threats, imprisonment, and even assassination for speaking out against corruption and injustice. These modern-day tyrants, like Jezebel, use fear and violence to maintain their grip on power and suppress any challenge to their authority. The killing of journalists and activists who expose the truth and stand up for justice is a stark reminder of how the spirit of Jezebel's cruelty lives on in contemporary society.

Moreover, Jezebel's ruthless slaying of the prophets underscores the dangers of unchecked power and the absence of accountability. When leaders have absolute power without any form of oversight, they can act with impunity, leading to widespread abuse and violence. This is why democratic institutions and mechanisms that promote transparency and accountability are essential in preventing such abuses of power. In today's world, efforts to ensure governmental accountability, protect human rights, and uphold the rule of law are crucial in preventing the kind of tyranny and violence exemplified by Jezebel's actions.

The story of Jezebel also highlights the importance of protecting and supporting those who are vulnerable to persecution. Just as some individuals took great risks to hide and protect the prophets from Jezebel's wrath, modern-day efforts to protect persecuted individuals and communities are vital. This includes providing asylum for refugees fleeing religious or political persecution, supporting human rights organizations, and advocating for policies that promote religious freedom and protect minority groups. The compassion and bravery shown by individuals and organizations that work to protect the persecuted are essential in countering the effects of oppressive actions similar to those carried out by Jezebel.

Furthermore, Jezebel's willingness to commit such atrocities to maintain her power reflects a broader theme of how leaders can become corrupted by their desire for control. This is evident in contemporary examples of leaders who go to great lengths, including committing human rights abuses, to retain their positions of power. The use of violence, propaganda, and coercion to suppress opposition and maintain control is a tactic that has been employed by many authoritarian regimes throughout history and continues to be a significant issue in many parts of the world today.

In conclusion, Jezebel's behavior as described in 1 Kings 18:13, where she ordered the slaying of the prophets of the Lord, is a stark example of the dangers of unchecked power, religious intolerance, and political persecution. Her actions forced individuals to take extraordinary measures to protect the innocent and uphold their faith. The parallels to modern-day instances of religious and political persecution, the importance of accountability and transparency, and the ongoing struggle for freedom and human rights highlight the enduring relevance of Jezebel's story. By reflecting on her actions and their consequences, we can better understand the critical importance of protecting religious and political freedoms, supporting those who are vulnerable to persecution, and ensuring that power is held accountable. The lessons from Jezebel's story serve as a timeless reminder of the need to promote justice, tolerance, and human dignity in our world today. Whether in ancient times or the present day, the need to stand against tyranny and protect the rights of individuals to express their beliefs and opinions remains as relevant as ever. The story of Jezebel is a powerful testament to the enduring struggle for justice and the importance of resisting oppressive forces in all their forms.

Chapter 4 -Sword

1 Kings 19:1 And Ahab told Jezebel all that Elijah had done, and withal how he had slain all the prophets with the sword.

Jezebel's behavior in the Bible is known for its ruthlessness and determination to maintain her power and influence, especially as seen in 1 Kings 19:1, where her actions lead to violence and the use of the sword. In this verse, King Ahab tells Jezebel about everything Elijah had done, including how he killed all the prophets of Baal with the sword. Instead of showing any remorse or reconsidering her ways, Jezebel responds with a vengeful threat, sending a message to Elijah that she intends to kill him in the same manner by the next day. Her reaction showcases her relentless pursuit of power and her willingness to use violence to achieve her goals. This kind of behavior can be compared to modern-day leaders and regimes that use force and intimidation to suppress opposition and maintain control.

In today's world, we can see similar behaviors in various forms of political and social violence. For instance, some authoritarian leaders use military and police forces to quash protests, silence dissent, and instill fear among the population. Just like Jezebel, these modern rulers resort to threats and actual violence to eliminate those who challenge their authority. This results in a climate of fear, where people are afraid to speak out against injustices or demand their rights, knowing that doing so could lead to severe consequences, including imprisonment, torture, or even death.

The use of the sword, or more broadly, the use of violence to achieve one's ends, is a tactic that has been employed throughout history and continues to be prevalent in many parts of the world today. For example, in some countries, government forces or militant groups engage in violent crackdowns against their own citizens, targeting activists, journalists, and political opponents. These actions are often justified as necessary for maintaining order or national security, but in reality, they are aimed at preserving the power of those in control. The violence and intimidation tactics used by these regimes are reminiscent of Jezebel's response to Elijah, where the threat of the sword was used to silence and eliminate opposition.

Furthermore, Jezebel's behavior highlights the dangers of a leadership that is driven by fear and vengeance rather than justice and compassion. Her willingness to use violence as a means to maintain her influence sets a dangerous precedent and perpetuates a cycle of violence and retribution. In contemporary society, we see similar patterns where leaders who prioritize their own power over the well-being of their people create environments of instability and conflict. This often leads to widespread suffering and injustice, as those in power use any means necessary, including violence, to suppress dissent and maintain their grip on authority.

The story of Jezebel and the use of the sword also underscore the importance of accountability and the rule of law in preventing such abuses of power. When leaders are not held accountable for their actions, they are more likely to resort to violent and oppressive measures to maintain control. This is why democratic institutions, checks and balances, and independent judicial systems are crucial in ensuring that those in power are held responsible for their actions and that justice is upheld. In many parts of the world, efforts to promote transparency, human rights, and the rule of law are essential in preventing the kind of tyranny and violence exemplified by Jezebel's actions.

Moreover, Jezebel's reaction to Elijah's victory over the prophets of Baal highlights the conflict between good and evil, truth and falsehood. Elijah's triumph represented a victory for the true God and the principles of justice and righteousness, while Jezebel's response embodied the forces of falsehood and oppression. This eternal struggle between good and evil continues to play out in today's world, where individuals and groups stand up against injustice and tyranny, often at great personal risk. The courage and determination of those who fight for truth and justice, much like Elijah, serve as a powerful reminder of the importance of standing up for what is right, even in the face of great danger.

Additionally, Jezebel's use of the sword can be seen as a metaphor for the destructive power of hatred and vengeance. When leaders or individuals act out of a desire for revenge, they often cause harm not only to their intended targets but also to innocent people and society as a whole. This cycle of violence and retribution creates an environment of fear and mistrust, where people are constantly looking over their shoulders, afraid of being the next target. In contrast, leadership based on principles of forgiveness, reconciliation, and justice can help to heal divisions and build stronger, more resilient communities.

The parallels between Jezebel's actions and modern-day uses of violence to maintain power also highlight the ongoing need for vigilance and advocacy in protecting human rights and promoting peace. Organizations and individuals around the world work tirelessly to expose abuses of power, support victims of violence, and advocate for policies that promote justice and equality. Their efforts are crucial in countering the forces of oppression and violence and in building a world where the rule of law prevails and human dignity is respected.

In conclusion, Jezebel's behavior as described in 1 Kings 19:1, where she responds to Elijah's actions with a vengeful threat of the sword, provides a stark example of the dangers of unchecked power and the use of violence to maintain control. Her actions mirror those of modern-day leaders and regimes that use force and intimidation to suppress opposition and perpetuate their rule. The story of Jezebel serves as a powerful reminder of the importance of accountability, the rule of law, and the need to stand up against tyranny and injustice. By reflecting on her actions and their consequences, we can better understand the critical importance of promoting justice, human rights, and the principles of peace and reconciliation in our own time.

Whether in ancient times or today, the lessons from Jezebel's story remain relevant and important for building a just and compassionate society. The ongoing struggle for truth and justice, and the need to resist the forces of oppression and violence, are as crucial now as they were in the days of Jezebel and Elijah.

Chapter 5 – Sent

1Kings 19:2 "Then Jezebel sent a messenger unto Elijah, saying, So let the gods do to me, and more also, if I make not thy life as the life of one of them by to morrow about this time."

In the Bible, Jezebel's behavior is particularly infamous in 1 Kings 19:2, where her actions reveal her ruthless and vengeful nature. After hearing about how Elijah had killed all the prophets of Baal, Jezebel sent a messenger to Elijah with a deadly threat, saying that by the next day, he would be dead just like the prophets he had slain. This act of sending a threat shows her determination to use fear and intimidation to maintain her power and silence those who opposed her. Jezebel's willingness to send a messenger with such a violent message highlights her manipulative and controlling character. She was not content with merely being angry; she actively sought to instill terror in Elijah, hoping to crush his spirit and stop his mission. This behavior is a stark example of how some people use threats and intimidation to control others and maintain their authority.

In today's world, we see similar behaviors in various forms, where individuals or leaders send threats to silence opposition and maintain control. For instance, in the political arena, there are cases where dissenting voices are met with threats of violence or legal action to intimidate and suppress them. Just as Jezebel sent a message to Elijah to scare him into submission, modern-day leaders and powerful individuals often use threats to discourage activists, journalists, and political opponents from speaking out against corruption and injustice. These threats can come in the form of direct messages, public statements, or even through intermediaries, much like Jezebel's messenger.

Furthermore, the act of sending a threat can also be seen in the context of cyberbullying and online harassment. With the rise of social media and digital communication, it has become easier for individuals to send threatening messages anonymously or from a distance. Cyberbullies use the power of the internet to intimidate and harass others, often targeting those who stand up against injustice or express unpopular opinions. Just as Jezebel used her position of power to send a threatening message to Elijah, cyberbullies exploit the anonymity and reach of the internet to spread fear and silence their victims.

Jezebel's actions also reflect a broader pattern of behavior seen in authoritarian regimes, where those in power use intimidation and threats to maintain their grip on authority. In many countries, political leaders and government officials send clear messages to their citizens that dissent will not be tolerated. This can include threats of imprisonment, torture, or even death for those who dare to challenge the status quo. These modern-day Jezebels use the same tactics of fear and intimidation to control their populations and prevent any opposition from gaining momentum.

Additionally, Jezebel's willingness to send a death threat to Elijah underscores the extent to which she would go to protect her interests and beliefs. This mirrors the actions of extremist groups today that send threats to those who oppose their ideologies. Whether it is through direct threats of violence or more subtle forms of intimidation, these groups aim to silence any voices that contradict their worldview. Just as Jezebel sought to eliminate Elijah, extremists today target those who promote peace, tolerance, and understanding, hoping to create an environment where only their beliefs are allowed to flourish.

Moreover, Jezebel's behavior highlights the impact of toxic leadership and the use of fear as a tool of governance. Leaders who rule through fear and threats create a culture of silence and compliance, where people are too afraid to speak out or challenge authority. This can lead to a society where injustice and corruption thrive, as there are no checks on the power of those in charge. In contrast, leaders who inspire and encourage open dialogue and dissent create a healthier and more just society. The contrast between Jezebel's reign of terror and the potential for positive leadership underscores the importance of promoting values of respect, dialogue, and justice in today's world.

The story of Jezebel and her sending of a threatening message to Elijah also serves as a reminder of the resilience and courage required to stand up against such intimidation. Despite Jezebel's threats, Elijah continued his mission, showing that fear tactics can be overcome with determination and faith. In contemporary times, this is seen in the bravery of activists, whistleblowers, and ordinary citizens who, despite facing threats and intimidation, continue to fight for justice and truth. Their courage in the face of danger is a powerful testament to the human spirit's resilience and the importance of standing up against oppression.

Furthermore, Jezebel's actions in sending a threat can also be seen in the context of workplace harassment, where managers or colleagues use threats to manipulate or control others. This can include threats of job loss, demotion, or other forms of punishment to coerce employees into compliance or silence. Just as Jezebel used her power to intimidate Elijah, workplace bullies use their positions of authority to instill fear and maintain control over their subordinates. Addressing such behavior requires creating a culture of respect and support, where individuals feel safe to speak out against harassment and intimidation without fear of retribution.

In conclusion, Jezebel's behavior in 1 Kings 19:2, where she sent a threatening message to Elijah, provides a vivid example of how fear and intimidation are used to maintain power and control. Her actions reflect a broader pattern of behavior seen in various forms of oppression and harassment in today's world, from political intimidation and cyberbullying to workplace harassment and extremist threats. By understanding and reflecting on Jezebel's actions, we can better recognize the importance of promoting justice, respect, and open dialogue in our own lives and societies. The lessons from Jezebel's story serve as a powerful reminder of the dangers of unchecked power and the need to stand up against fear and intimidation to build a just and compassionate world. Whether in ancient times or today, the struggle against oppression and the fight for justice and truth remain as relevant and crucial as ever. The resilience and courage of those who stand up against threats and intimidation, much like Elijah, continue to inspire and remind us of the enduring power of the human spirit to overcome fear and promote positive change.

Chapter 6 – Sad

1Kings 21:5 "But Jezebel his wife came to him, and said unto him, Why is thy spirit so sad, that thou eatest no bread?"

Jezebel's behavior in the Bible, especially as described in 1 Kings 21:5, provides a stark illustration of her manipulative and controlling nature, and offers numerous parallels to modern-day behavior in various aspects of life. In this verse, Jezebel notices that her husband, King Ahab, is unusually sad and refuses to eat. Concerned about his mood, she asks him why he is so sad and why he isn't eating. Ahab then tells her that he is upset because Naboth, a common man, refused to sell him his vineyard. Instead of comforting Ahab or respecting Naboth's rights, Jezebel sees an opportunity to manipulate the situation to her advantage. She immediately takes charge, devising a plan to falsely accuse Naboth of blasphemy, which ultimately leads to his unjust execution, allowing Ahab to seize the vineyard. Jezebel's response to Ahab's sadness is not one of empathy or understanding, but rather a calculated move to gain power and satisfy her husband's desires through deceit and manipulation. This behavior can be compared to various modern scenarios where people in positions of power or influence exploit the vulnerabilities or emotions of others to achieve their own goals.

In today's world, similar manipulative behaviors can be observed in many areas, including politics, business, and personal relationships. For instance, in the political arena, some leaders exploit the emotions and fears of their constituents to push through their agendas. They use propaganda, misinformation, and deceitful tactics to manipulate public opinion and maintain control, much like Jezebel manipulated Ahab's sadness to orchestrate Naboth's demise. This manipulation often leads to unjust policies and actions that benefit the few at the expense of the many, mirroring the way Jezebel's scheme led to Naboth's wrongful death and the seizure of his property.

In the business world, leaders or managers may exploit the emotions or weaknesses of their employees to achieve their own ends. This could involve using manipulative tactics to push through unpopular decisions, coercing employees into overworking or accepting unfair conditions, or taking advantage of their vulnerabilities to maintain control. Just as Jezebel saw Ahab's sadness as an opportunity to act deceitfully, some modern-day business leaders see their employees' concerns or vulnerabilities as chances to assert their authority and benefit themselves or their companies, often leading to toxic work environments and unjust practices.

On a personal level, manipulative behavior similar to Jezebel's can be found in relationships where one person exploits the emotions of another to gain control or fulfill their desires. This can happen in friendships, romantic relationships, or even within families. For example, a person might use guilt, sadness, or other emotions to manipulate their partner into doing something they wouldn't otherwise agree to, thereby gaining power and control in the relationship. This kind of emotional manipulation can lead to unhealthy dynamics and can be deeply damaging, just as Jezebel's manipulation led to a tragic and unjust outcome for Naboth.

Moreover, Jezebel's actions in 1 Kings 21:5 highlight the dangers of unchecked power and the lengths to which people will go to achieve their desires when they feel entitled to do so. Her ability to manipulate Ahab's sadness into a deadly plot against Naboth underscores the importance of ethical leadership and the need for accountability. In contemporary society, the absence of such accountability can result in abuses of power, corruption, and widespread injustice. Leaders in any capacity—whether in government, business, or personal relationships—must be held accountable for their actions to prevent the kind of manipulation and abuse exemplified by Jezebel's behavior.

Jezebel's story also serves as a cautionary tale about the impact of manipulation and deceit on individuals and communities. Her actions led to the wrongful death of an innocent man and the unjust seizure of his property, creating a legacy of cruelty and injustice. In modern times, similar manipulative behaviors can lead to significant harm, including the erosion of trust, the breakdown of communities, and the perpetuation of inequality and injustice. It is crucial to recognize and address manipulative behaviors to build fairer, more just societies.

Furthermore, Jezebel's response to Ahab's sadness illustrates a profound lack of empathy and moral integrity. Instead of addressing the root of Ahab's emotional distress or seeking a fair resolution, she chose a path of deceit and violence. This lack of empathy and disregard for ethical considerations is something we still see today in various forms. For example, some leaders and influencers prioritize their own interests over the well-being of others, leading to decisions and actions that harm individuals and communities. The absence of empathy and ethical integrity in leadership can result in policies and practices that are unjust and detrimental to society.

The story of Jezebel and her manipulative response to Ahab's sadness also underscores the importance of ethical decision-making and the need for leaders to act with integrity and compassion. In all areas of life, from politics to business to personal relationships, decisions should be made with consideration for their impact on others, and with a commitment to fairness and justice. By prioritizing empathy and ethical behavior, leaders can prevent the kind of manipulative and destructive actions exemplified by Jezebel's response to Ahab's sadness.

In conclusion, Jezebel's behavior as described in 1 Kings 21:5, where she manipulates Ahab's sadness to achieve her own ends, provides a powerful example of the dangers of manipulative and unethical behavior. Her actions led to the wrongful death of Naboth and the unjust seizure of his property, highlighting the devastating impact of such behavior. The parallels to modern-day scenarios in politics, business, and personal relationships underscore the enduring relevance of this story and the importance of ethical leadership and accountability. By reflecting on Jezebel's actions and their consequences, we can better understand the need to promote empathy, integrity, and justice in all areas of life. The lessons from Jezebel's story serve as a timeless reminder of the importance of acting with compassion and ethical integrity to build a just and fair society. Whether in ancient times or today, the need to recognize and address manipulative behaviors, and to hold leaders accountable for their actions, remains as crucial as ever. The ongoing struggle for justice and the promotion of ethical leadership are vital for preventing the kind of harm and injustice exemplified by Jezebel's manipulative and deceitful actions.

Chapter 7 – Scheming

I Kings 21:7 "And Jezebel his wife said unto him, Dost thou now govern the kingdom of Israel? arise, and eat bread, and let thine heart be merry: I will give thee the vineyard of Naboth the Jezreelite."

In the Bible, Jezebel's behavior is often depicted as cunning and scheming, especially in 1 Kings 21:7, where she takes charge of a situation to get what she wants by any means necessary. In this verse, Ahab, the King of Israel, is upset because Naboth refuses to sell him his vineyard. Jezebel, seeing her husband's distress, schemes to solve the problem in a way that shows her manipulative and ruthless nature. She tells Ahab to cheer up and eat, assuring him that she will get him the vineyard of Naboth the Jezreelite. Jezebel then devises a plan to falsely accuse Naboth of blasphemy and treason, leading to his execution and enabling Ahab to take possession of the vineyard. Her actions highlight her willingness to use deceit and manipulation to achieve her goals, regardless of the moral or ethical implications. Jezebel's scheming behavior in this context can be compared to various modern-day scenarios where individuals or leaders use cunning and dishonest tactics to get what they want.

In today's world, we see similar scheming behaviors in politics, business, and personal relationships. In politics, some leaders and politicians engage in deceitful strategies to gain power or push their agendas. This can include spreading false information, manipulating facts, or using underhanded tactics to discredit opponents. Just as Jezebel schemed to falsely accuse Naboth, modern politicians might fabricate stories or use smear campaigns to undermine their rivals and sway public opinion in their favor. This kind of political scheming can lead to a loss of trust in public institutions and erode democratic processes, creating an environment where unethical behavior becomes normalized.

In the business world, scheming behaviors can also be observed when companies or individuals engage in unethical practices to gain a competitive edge. This might involve insider trading, manipulating financial reports, or engaging in fraudulent activities to deceive stakeholders and increase profits. Like Jezebel's scheme to get Naboth's vineyard, these business practices often involve deceit and a disregard for the well-being of others. The consequences can be far-reaching, affecting not only the immediate victims but also the broader economy and public trust in corporate institutions. Scandals involving major corporations, where executives scheme to hide losses or inflate profits, serve as modern parallels to Jezebel's manipulative tactics.

In personal relationships, scheming behavior can manifest in various ways, such as manipulating friends, family members, or romantic partners to achieve personal goals. This can include lying, spreading rumors, or using emotional manipulation to control others and get what one wants. Jezebel's manipulation of Ahab to achieve her goal of acquiring Naboth's vineyard mirrors how individuals might use deceitful tactics to influence and control those close to them. This kind of behavior can lead to broken relationships, loss of trust, and emotional harm, highlighting the destructive impact of scheming on a personal level.

Moreover, Jezebel's scheming actions highlight the dangers of unchecked ambition and the lengths to which individuals will go to achieve their desires. Her willingness to use false accusations and have an innocent man killed for personal gain underscores the importance of ethical boundaries and the need to hold individuals accountable for their actions. In contemporary society, the absence of accountability can lead to widespread corruption and abuse of power. Ensuring that leaders and individuals are held responsible for their actions is crucial in preventing the kind of scheming and manipulation exemplified by Jezebel's behavior.

The story of Jezebel also serves as a cautionary tale about the impact of scheming and deceit on communities and societies. Her actions led to the unjust death of Naboth and the seizure of his property, creating a legacy of injustice and cruelty. In modern times, similar scheming behaviors can lead to significant harm, including social unrest, economic instability, and the erosion of public trust. Recognizing and addressing scheming behavior is essential in building fairer and more just societies. This involves promoting transparency, integrity, and accountability in all areas of life, from politics and business to personal relationships.

Furthermore, Jezebel's behavior illustrates the importance of ethical decision-making and the need for leaders to act with integrity and compassion. Decisions made through deceit and manipulation often lead to negative consequences and can harm innocent people. In contrast, ethical leadership involves making decisions based on fairness, honesty, and respect for others. By prioritizing ethical behavior, leaders can prevent the kind of harm caused by Jezebel's scheming and build stronger, more resilient communities.

The parallels between Jezebel's actions and modern-day scheming also highlight the ongoing need for vigilance and advocacy in protecting human rights and promoting justice. Organizations and individuals around the world work tirelessly to expose corrupt practices, support victims of injustice, and advocate for policies that promote fairness and equality. Their efforts are crucial in countering the forces of deceit and manipulation and in building a world where ethical behavior is valued and rewarded.

In conclusion, Jezebel's behavior as described in 1 Kings 21:7, where she schemes to acquire Naboth's vineyard through deceit and manipulation, provides a powerful example of the dangers of unethical behavior and the lengths to which individuals will go to achieve their desires. Her actions led to the wrongful death of Naboth and the unjust seizure of his property, highlighting the devastating impact of such behavior. The parallels to modern-day scenarios in politics, business, and personal relationships underscore the enduring relevance of this story and the importance of ethical leadership and accountability. By reflecting on Jezebel's actions and their consequences, we can better understand the need to promote transparency, integrity, and justice in all areas of life. The lessons from Jezebel's story serve as a timeless reminder of the importance of acting with compassion and ethical integrity to build a just and fair society. Whether in ancient times or today, the need to recognize and address scheming behaviors, and to hold individuals accountable for their actions, remains as crucial as ever. The ongoing struggle for justice and the promotion of ethical leadership are vital for preventing the kind of harm and injustice exemplified by Jezebel's manipulative and deceitful actions. By fostering a culture of honesty, accountability, and respect, we can work towards a world where ethical behavior is the norm, and the destructive impact of scheming is minimized.

Chapter 8 – Subordinates

I Kings 21:11 And the men of his city, even the elders and the nobles who were the inhabitants in his city, did as Jezebel had sent unto them, and as it was written in the letters which she had sent unto them.

Jezebel's behavior as depicted in the Bible, particularly in 1 Kings 21:11, showcases her manipulative and authoritarian nature, as she uses her subordinates to carry out her nefarious plans. In this verse, Jezebel writes letters in Ahab's name and sends them to the elders and nobles who lived in Naboth's city, instructing them to proclaim a fast and set Naboth in a prominent place among the people. She further orders them to find two scoundrels to bring false charges against Naboth, accusing him of cursing both God and the king. Following her orders, the subordinates comply without question, leading to Naboth's wrongful execution by stoning. This incident highlights how Jezebel manipulates her subordinates, exploiting their positions and obedience to achieve her sinister goals. Her ability to bend others to her will without resistance shows her dominance and the fear she instilled in those who served under her.

In today's world, similar behaviors can be observed in various settings where leaders or people in power manipulate their subordinates to fulfill unethical or illegal actions. This can be seen in corporate environments where executives may pressure employees to engage in fraudulent activities, such as falsifying financial records or engaging in insider trading, to protect the company's image or increase profits. Just as Jezebel's subordinates carried out her deceitful plan without questioning her motives, modern employees might feel compelled to follow unethical directives from their superiors due to fear of losing their jobs or facing other repercussions. This culture of compliance and fear can lead to significant harm, including financial scandals, loss of public trust, and legal consequences for the company and individuals involved.

Similarly, in political arenas, leaders may use their influence over subordinates to implement corrupt practices, suppress dissent, or manipulate public opinion. For instance, government officials might be ordered to overlook legal procedures, fabricate evidence, or engage in voter suppression to maintain the ruling party's power. These subordinates, much like the elders and nobles in Naboth's city, may comply due to loyalty, fear, or personal gain, perpetuating a cycle of corruption and injustice. The misuse of power in this way undermines democratic institutions and erodes public confidence in governance, leading to widespread disillusionment and unrest.

In personal relationships, manipulative individuals might exploit the loyalty and trust of their friends, family members, or partners to achieve their selfish objectives. For example, a person might pressure their partner to lie or deceive others to protect their interests or to avoid consequences. This type of manipulation can create toxic dynamics, where individuals feel trapped and coerced into actions they know are wrong, mirroring the coercive influence Jezebel wielded over her subordinates. The emotional and psychological toll of such manipulation can be profound, leading to strained relationships and long-term mental health issues for those involved.

Moreover, Jezebel's actions in 1 Kings 21:11 also highlight the broader theme of how individuals in positions of power can corrupt and compromise the integrity of those who serve under them. When leaders prioritize their selfish desires over ethical considerations, they can create an environment where wrongdoing becomes normalized and accepted. This corruption of values not only affects the immediate victims, such as Naboth, but also has a ripple effect on the broader community, undermining social cohesion and trust.

The story of Jezebel and her manipulation of subordinates also serves as a cautionary tale about the importance of moral courage and integrity. The elders and nobles who carried out Jezebel's orders could have refused to participate in the deceitful plot, choosing to stand up for justice and truth. In contemporary society, individuals in subordinate positions often face similar ethical dilemmas, where they must decide whether to comply with unethical directives or to take a stand against wrongdoing. Promoting a culture of integrity and encouraging individuals to speak out against unethical practices are crucial in preventing the kind of manipulation and abuse exemplified by Jezebel's actions.

Furthermore, Jezebel's behavior illustrates the potential consequences of unchecked power and the lack of accountability. When leaders are not held accountable for their actions, they can misuse their power to manipulate and exploit those around them. This absence of accountability can lead to a culture of impunity, where unethical behavior is tolerated and even encouraged. Ensuring that leaders at all levels are held responsible for their actions is essential in fostering an environment where ethical behavior is upheld, and justice is served.

The parallels between Jezebel's actions and modern-day scenarios also underscore the need for robust systems of oversight and accountability in all areas of society. Whether in corporate governance, political institutions, or personal relationships, mechanisms that promote transparency and accountability are vital in preventing the abuse of power. By establishing clear ethical guidelines and ensuring that those who violate them are held accountable, societies can protect individuals from manipulation and exploitation.

In conclusion, Jezebel's behavior as described in 1 Kings 21:11, where she manipulates her subordinates to carry out a deceitful and deadly plan, provides a powerful example of the dangers of unchecked power and the corrupting influence of unethical leadership. Her actions led to the wrongful death of Naboth and the seizure of his property, highlighting the devastating impact of manipulative and authoritarian behavior. The parallels to modern-day scenarios in politics, business, and personal relationships underscore the enduring relevance of this story and the importance of ethical leadership and accountability. By reflecting on Jezebel's actions and their consequences, we can better understand the need to promote integrity, moral courage, and accountability in all areas of life. The lessons from Jezebel's story serve as a timeless reminder of the importance of standing up against manipulation and abuse, fostering a culture of ethical behavior, and ensuring that those in positions of power are held accountable for their actions. Whether in ancient times or today, the need to recognize and address manipulative behaviors and to protect individuals from exploitation remains as crucial as ever. The ongoing struggle for justice, integrity, and ethical leadership is vital for building a just and compassionate society, where the rights and dignity of all individuals are respected and upheld. By promoting transparency, accountability, and moral courage, we can work towards a world where ethical behavior is the norm and the destructive impact of manipulation and deceit is minimized.

Chapter 9 – Stoned

I Kings 21:14 Then they sent to Jezebel, saying, Naboth is stoned, and is dead.

In 1 Kings 21:14, Jezebel's behavior is depicted in one of the most chilling and ruthless actions she orchestrated. After she concocted a scheme to accuse Naboth falsely of blasphemy and treason, the elders and nobles of Naboth's city carried out her orders, and they sent word to Jezebel saying, "Naboth has been stoned and is dead." This verse shows the culmination of Jezebel's manipulative and evil plan to secure Naboth's vineyard for her husband, King Ahab. Her actions led to the brutal execution of an innocent man through stoning, a public and painful method of capital punishment. This highlights Jezebel's willingness to go to extreme lengths, including murder, to achieve her selfish goals. Her use of false accusations and exploitation of her power to have Naboth stoned to death mirrors many modern-day situations where individuals or groups use lies, manipulation, and violence to get what they want.

In today's world, similar behaviors can be seen in various contexts, such as political, corporate, and social spheres. For example, in some countries, political leaders or parties might resort to fabricating charges against their opponents to eliminate competition and secure their own power. Just as Jezebel falsely accused Naboth, modern politicians might use smear campaigns, false evidence, or corrupt legal systems to imprison or discredit their rivals. These actions undermine the integrity of political systems, leading to a climate of fear and injustice where the rule of law is replaced by the rule of the powerful.

In the corporate world, executives or companies may engage in unethical practices to eliminate competition or protect their interests. This can include spreading false information about competitors, manipulating markets, or using legal loopholes to undermine rivals. Such behavior, reminiscent of Jezebel's scheming to have Naboth stoned, can lead to significant harm, including financial losses, damaged reputations, and a lack of trust in the business environment. The stoning of Naboth serves as a stark reminder of the destructive impact of such ruthless and unethical practices.

Socially, individuals or groups might resort to character assassination, bullying, or harassment to achieve their goals or to silence dissenting voices. For instance, in the age of social media, false accusations and targeted harassment campaigns can be used to ruin someone's reputation or career. Just as Naboth was stoned based on false charges, people today can be metaphorically "stoned" through the spread of lies and misinformation, leading to social ostracism, mental distress, and sometimes even driving victims to extreme actions like suicide. The anonymity and reach of the internet make it easier for such modern-day "stonings" to occur, often with devastating consequences.

Jezebel's actions also highlight the dangers of unchecked power and the absence of accountability. Her ability to have Naboth stoned to death without facing any immediate consequences shows how power can be abused when there are no checks and balances. In contemporary society, this can be seen in instances where leaders or influential individuals act with impunity, knowing that their positions protect them from repercussions. This lack of accountability can lead to widespread corruption, human rights abuses, and a breakdown of trust in institutions. Ensuring that those in power are held accountable for their actions is crucial in preventing the kind of abuses exemplified by Jezebel's behavior.

Moreover, the stoning of Naboth underscores the importance of standing up against injustice and defending the innocent. The elders and nobles who carried out Jezebel's orders did so without questioning the morality or legality of their actions. This reflects a broader issue of compliance and the failure to speak out against wrongdoing. In modern times, this can be seen in various scenarios where individuals or groups fail to challenge unethical practices or injustices, whether due to fear, apathy, or complicity. Encouraging a culture of ethical behavior and moral courage is essential in preventing such abuses and ensuring that justice is upheld.

The story of Jezebel and Naboth also serves as a reminder of the potential consequences of false accusations. Naboth's unjust death due to false charges of blasphemy and treason mirrors the impact of wrongful accusations today, which can lead to wrongful imprisonment, loss of reputation, and even death. The ease with which Jezebel was able to manipulate the system to have Naboth stoned highlights the need for robust legal protections and due process to prevent miscarriages of justice. In contemporary legal systems, ensuring that accusations are thoroughly investigated and that individuals have the right to a fair trial is crucial in protecting against similar injustices.

Furthermore, Jezebel's manipulation of the legal and social systems to achieve her ends illustrates the pervasive nature of corruption and the abuse of power. Her actions not only resulted in Naboth's death but also set a precedent for how power could be wielded to destroy lives and property. In today's world, combating corruption and ensuring that power is used responsibly and ethically is vital in promoting justice and social stability. This involves implementing and enforcing anti-corruption measures, promoting transparency, and holding those in positions of power accountable for their actions.

The parallels between Jezebel's actions and modern-day behaviors also underscore the importance of vigilance and advocacy in protecting human rights and promoting justice. Organizations and individuals who work to expose corruption, defend the innocent, and advocate for legal and social reforms play a crucial role in countering the forces of deceit and manipulation. Their efforts help to build a world where justice prevails, and the rights and dignity of all individuals are respected and upheld.

In conclusion, Jezebel's behavior as described in 1 Kings 21:14, where she orchestrates the stoning of Naboth through false accusations and manipulation, provides a powerful example of the dangers of unchecked power and the destructive impact of unethical behavior. Her actions led to the wrongful death of an innocent man, highlighting the devastating consequences of such ruthless and deceitful practices. The parallels to modern-day scenarios in politics, business, and social contexts underscore the enduring relevance of this story and the importance of ethical leadership and accountability. By reflecting on Jezebel's actions and their consequences, we can better understand the need to promote integrity, moral courage, and justice in all areas of life. The lessons from Jezebel's story serve as a timeless reminder of the importance of standing up against manipulation, false accusations, and abuse of power, fostering a culture of ethical behavior, and ensuring that those in positions of authority are held accountable for their actions. Whether in ancient times or today, the need to recognize and address manipulative and unethical behaviors, and to protect individuals from exploitation and injustice, remains as crucial as ever. The ongoing struggle for justice, integrity, and ethical leadership is vital for building a just and compassionate society, where the rights and dignity of all individuals are respected and upheld. By promoting transparency, accountability, and moral courage, we can work towards a world where ethical behavior is the norm, and the destructive impact of manipulation and deceit is minimized.

Chapter 10 – Seizing

I Kings 21:15 And it came to pass, when Jezebel heard that Naboth was stoned, and was dead, that Jezebel said to Ahab, Arise, take possession of the vineyard of Naboth the Jezreelite, which he refused to give thee for money: for Naboth is not alive, but dead.

In 1 Kings 21:15, Jezebel's behavior is vividly depicted as she coldly seizes the opportunity to consolidate her and Ahab's power by taking possession of Naboth's vineyard. After hearing that Naboth has been stoned to death, Jezebel informs Ahab, saying, "Get up and take possession of the vineyard of Naboth the Jezreelite that he refused to sell you. He is no longer alive but dead." This verse illustrates Jezebel's ruthless and calculating nature, as she not only orchestrated Naboth's unjust execution but also promptly moved to seize his property. Her actions reflect a complete disregard for justice and human life, focusing solely on achieving her own goals and satisfying Ahab's desires. Jezebel's seizing of Naboth's vineyard after his murder can be compared to numerous modern-day scenarios where powerful individuals or groups exploit their positions to illegitimately acquire property, wealth, or power.

In today's world, similar behaviors are often observed in political and corporate arenas, where leaders and influential figures use their power to seize assets and control resources unethically. For example, in some corrupt political regimes, leaders might confiscate land, businesses, or personal property from their opponents or the public under false pretenses, much like Jezebel orchestrated the death of Naboth to claim his vineyard. This abuse of power undermines the rule of law and perpetuates a climate of fear and injustice. People may lose their homes, livelihoods, and even their lives due to the unscrupulous actions of those in power who are driven by greed and a desire for control.

In the corporate world, unethical practices can involve hostile takeovers, where powerful companies use aggressive tactics to acquire smaller businesses, often disregarding the well-being of employees and the ethical implications of their actions. These corporate takeovers can resemble Jezebel's seizing of Naboth's vineyard, as they often involve manipulative strategies and exploitation of legal loopholes to achieve their objectives. Such practices can lead to job losses, reduced competition, and negative impacts on local communities, highlighting the far-reaching consequences of unethical business behavior.

On a more personal level, individuals may also engage in behaviors that reflect Jezebel's seizing of Naboth's property. This can occur in familial or social contexts where people manipulate or deceive others to gain control over assets or resources. For instance, family members might use coercion or deceit to alter wills, gain control of family businesses, or acquire property. These actions create divisions, foster resentment, and perpetuate cycles of conflict and mistrust within families and communities.

Jezebel's behavior also sheds light on the broader issue of land and resource grabbing, which continues to be a significant problem in many parts of the world. Powerful individuals, corporations, or governments often seize land and resources from vulnerable populations, displacing communities and disrupting livelihoods. These actions are frequently justified through legal or bureaucratic means, but they mirror the unjust and ruthless seizure of Naboth's vineyard. The impact on affected communities can be devastating, leading to poverty, loss of cultural heritage, and social instability.

Moreover, Jezebel's actions highlight the dangers of unchecked ambition and the ethical void that can accompany the pursuit of power. Her willingness to go to such lengths to satisfy Ahab's desires reflects a broader theme of how ambition, when left unchecked, can lead to moral corruption and abuse of power. In contemporary society, this is evident in various scenarios where individuals prioritize their own ambitions over ethical considerations, leading to harmful consequences for others. Whether in politics, business, or personal relationships, the drive for power and control can result in actions that are detrimental to the broader community.

The story of Jezebel and her seizing of Naboth's vineyard also underscores the importance of legal and ethical safeguards to prevent the abuse of power. Robust legal frameworks and transparent governance are crucial in protecting individuals and communities from exploitation and ensuring that justice prevails. In many parts of the world, efforts to strengthen legal protections for property rights, promote transparency, and combat corruption are essential in preventing scenarios similar to Jezebel's ruthless actions.

Furthermore, Jezebel's manipulation of legal and social systems to achieve her ends serves as a reminder of the need for vigilance and advocacy in defending the rights of the vulnerable. Organizations and individuals dedicated to human rights and social justice play a critical role in exposing and challenging abuses of power, advocating for legal reforms, and supporting those who are affected by unjust practices. Their work helps to build a more just and equitable society, where the rights and dignity of all individuals are respected.

The parallels between Jezebel's actions and modern-day behaviors also highlight the ongoing struggle for justice and the importance of ethical leadership. Leaders who act with integrity, prioritize the well-being of others, and adhere to ethical principles can help to prevent the kind of exploitation and abuse exemplified by Jezebel's behavior. Promoting a culture of accountability, transparency, and respect for the rule of law is vital in creating environments where power is exercised responsibly and ethically.

In conclusion, Jezebel's behavior as described in 1 Kings 21:15, where she seizes Naboth's vineyard after orchestrating his death, provides a powerful example of the dangers of unchecked ambition and the abuse of power. Her actions led to the wrongful death of an innocent man and the unjust acquisition of his property, highlighting the devastating impact of such ruthless and unethical practices. The parallels to modern-day scenarios in politics, business, and personal contexts underscore the enduring relevance of this story and the importance of ethical leadership and accountability. By reflecting on Jezebel's actions and their consequences, we can better understand the need to promote integrity, moral courage, and justice in all areas of life. The lessons from Jezebel's story serve as a timeless reminder of the importance of standing up against exploitation, fostering a culture of ethical behavior, and ensuring that those in positions of authority are held accountable for their actions. Whether in ancient times or today, the need to recognize and address manipulative and unethical behaviors, and to protect individuals from exploitation and injustice, remains as crucial as ever. The ongoing struggle for justice, integrity, and ethical leadership is vital for building a just and compassionate society, where the rights and dignity of all individuals are respected and upheld. By promoting transparency, accountability, and moral courage, we can work towards a world where ethical behavior is the norm, and the destructive impact of manipulation and deceit is minimized. This story reminds us that the fight against injustice and the promotion of ethical leadership are ongoing efforts that require the commitment and vigilance of everyone in society.

Chapter 11 – The Sentencing

I Kings 21:23 And of Jezebel also spake the LORD, saying, The dogs shall eat Jezebel by the wall of Jezreel.

In 1 Kings 21:23, Jezebel's behavior leads to a significant and chilling prophecy about her ultimate fate, serving as a divine sentence for her numerous wrongdoings. This sentence was pronounced by Elijah the prophet as a judgment from God for Jezebel's evil actions, particularly her role in the unjust death of Naboth and the widespread idolatry and corruption she fostered in Israel. This prophetic sentence highlights the inevitable consequences of Jezebel's ruthless, manipulative, and immoral behavior, signaling that justice, although delayed, would ultimately prevail. In today's world, similar behaviors are observed when powerful individuals or leaders act unethically or illegally, believing they are above the law, only to eventually face the consequences of their actions, whether through legal systems, public backlash, or divine justice.

Jezebel's sentence is reflective of the broader principle that unethical actions, particularly those involving abuse of power and corruption, often lead to downfall and retribution. In contemporary society, many political leaders, business executives, and influential figures engage in activities similar to Jezebel's, such as corruption, manipulation, and exploitation, believing they can evade accountability due to their power and influence. However, history and current events show that such individuals often face significant consequences, whether through legal prosecution, loss of reputation, or other forms of justice. For example, political scandals involving corruption and abuse of power frequently result in investigations, trials, and, in many cases, imprisonment for those involved. These modern parallels to Jezebel's story underscore the importance of accountability and the idea that justice, though sometimes slow, eventually catches up with wrongdoers.

In the corporate world, executives who engage in fraudulent activities or unethical business practices often face severe repercussions, including legal penalties, financial losses, and damage to their reputations. The downfall of powerful figures in major corporations due to scandals involving embezzlement, insider trading, or environmental violations mirrors the downfall prophesied for Jezebel. These cases highlight how the pursuit of personal gain at the expense of ethical conduct can lead to significant consequences, reinforcing the principle that unethical behavior is ultimately unsustainable.

On a personal level, individuals who manipulate, deceive, or exploit others in their personal relationships may also face similar consequences. Just as Jezebel's actions led to a divine sentence predicting her gruesome end, people who engage in unethical behavior in their personal lives often experience the breakdown of relationships, loss of trust, and social ostracism. This can manifest in various forms, such as being exposed for their actions, losing the respect of peers and loved ones, or facing legal consequences for any crimes committed. The story of Jezebel serves as a reminder that personal integrity and ethical behavior are crucial in maintaining healthy and trusting relationships.

Furthermore, Jezebel's sentence highlights the concept of divine justice, where moral and ethical breaches are met with retribution from a higher power. This idea resonates in many cultures and religions, where there is a belief that ultimate justice is administered by a divine entity, ensuring that wrongdoers are held accountable for their actions. In contemporary society, this concept is often reflected in the idea of karma or the belief that good and bad actions will eventually return to the individual in kind. People who engage in harmful or unethical behavior may find themselves facing consequences that seem to be the result of a higher moral order, reinforcing the belief that justice is a universal principle.

The story of Jezebel and her sentence also underscores the importance of ethical leadership and the role of accountability in governance. Leaders who abuse their power and act unethically create environments of fear, corruption, and injustice. Ensuring that such leaders are held accountable is crucial in maintaining the integrity of institutions and promoting a culture of justice and fairness. Modern systems of governance emphasize the need for checks and balances, transparency, and the rule of law to prevent the abuse of power and ensure that leaders are accountable for their actions. This is reflected in the prosecution of corrupt officials, the implementation of anti-corruption measures, and the promotion of ethical standards in leadership.

Moreover, the prophetic sentence against Jezebel serves as a warning about the long-term consequences of unethical behavior. While individuals like Jezebel may temporarily succeed in their schemes, their actions ultimately lead to their downfall. This principle can be applied to various aspects of life, reminding us that short-term gains achieved through unethical means are often outweighed by long-term repercussions. The downfall of Jezebel is a testament to the enduring truth that integrity and ethical behavior are foundational to sustainable success and fulfillment.

The parallels between Jezebel's story and modern-day scenarios also highlight the role of prophetic voices and whistleblowers in society. Just as Elijah pronounced the divine sentence against Jezebel, modern whistleblowers and activists often expose corruption, injustice, and unethical behavior, prompting accountability and change. These individuals play a critical role in upholding justice and integrity, often at great personal risk. Their courage and determination to speak out against wrongdoing are essential in promoting transparency and accountability in various sectors of society.

In conclusion, Jezebel's behavior as described in 1 Kings 21:23, where she receives a prophetic sentence of divine retribution, provides a powerful example of the consequences of unethical behavior and the abuse of power. Her actions led to a gruesome and inevitable downfall, highlighting the importance of accountability and the principle that justice, though sometimes delayed, ultimately prevails. The parallels to modern-day scenarios in politics, business, and personal contexts underscore the enduring relevance of this story and the importance of ethical leadership, accountability, and integrity. By reflecting on Jezebel's actions and their consequences, we can better understand the need to promote justice, transparency, and ethical behavior in all areas of life. The lessons from Jezebel's story serve as a timeless reminder of the importance of acting with integrity and the inevitability of justice for those who engage in unethical behavior. Whether in ancient times or today, the need to recognize and address manipulative and unethical behaviors, and to protect individuals from exploitation and injustice, remains as crucial as ever. The ongoing struggle for justice, integrity, and ethical leadership is vital for building a just and compassionate society, where the rights and dignity of all individuals are respected and upheld. By promoting transparency, accountability, and moral courage, we can work towards a world where ethical behavior is the norm, and the destructive impact of manipulation and deceit is minimized. This story reminds us that the fight against injustice and the promotion of ethical leadership are ongoing efforts that require the commitment and vigilance of everyone in society.

Chapter 12 – Stirred

I Kings 21:25 But there was none like unto Ahab, which did sell himself to work wickedness in the sight of the LORD, whom Jezebel his wife stirred up.

In 1 Kings 21:25, Jezebel's behavior is highlighted in a particularly damning way as it states, "But there was none like unto Ahab, which did sell himself to work wickedness in the sight of the Lord, whom Jezebel his wife stirred up." This verse emphasizes that Ahab, the King of Israel, was led to commit the worst kinds of evil by the influence and instigation of his wife, Jezebel. Her ability to stir up Ahab to do wrong showcases her manipulative and malevolent nature, as she constantly encouraged and provoked him to abandon his moral compass and engage in actions that were deeply offensive to God. Jezebel's role in stirring Ahab to commit such wickedness can be compared to modern-day scenarios where individuals or groups use their influence to incite others to engage in unethical or harmful behavior.

In contemporary society, similar behaviors can be observed in various contexts, including politics, corporate environments, and social interactions. For example, in the political arena, advisors or close associates of leaders may stir them up to pursue corrupt or oppressive policies for personal gain or ideological reasons. Just as Jezebel pushed Ahab towards evil deeds, modern political figures might be influenced by those around them to act against the interests of their people, leading to corruption, human rights abuses, and social unrest. These advisors or associates may manipulate leaders by playing on their fears, ambitions, or prejudices, encouraging them to take actions that harm others and undermine the integrity of their leadership.

In the corporate world, executives or managers can be stirred up by colleagues or business partners to engage in unethical practices such as fraud, embezzlement, or exploitation of workers. This often involves a combination of persuasion, manipulation, and pressure to achieve financial or competitive advantages. The stirring up of unethical behavior in a corporate setting can lead to significant consequences, including legal penalties, financial losses, and damage to the company's reputation. Employees may be coerced into actions that go against their values, creating a toxic work environment and perpetuating a culture of dishonesty and greed.

On a personal level, individuals may be influenced by peers or family members to engage in negative behaviors such as substance abuse, bullying, or criminal activities. Peer pressure and the desire to fit in can lead people, especially young individuals, to abandon their moral principles and participate in harmful activities. Jezebel's role in stirring Ahab to do evil is mirrored in these situations where one person's negative influence leads another to make destructive choices. The impact of such influence can be devastating, leading to broken relationships, legal troubles, and long-term personal harm.

Moreover, Jezebel's behavior underscores the broader theme of the power of influence and the responsibility that comes with it. Those who hold influence over others, whether in leadership positions, advisory roles, or as peers, have the power to shape decisions and actions significantly. This influence can be used for good or ill, and the story of Jezebel serves as a cautionary tale about the consequences of using influence to promote wickedness and immorality. In modern times, the responsibility of influencers, be they political leaders, corporate executives, or social media personalities, to use their power ethically and positively is paramount.

Jezebel's ability to stir Ahab into committing evil also highlights the importance of personal integrity and the strength to resist negative influences. Ahab's weakness in succumbing to Jezebel's provocations serves as a reminder that individuals must hold fast to their moral values and principles, even when faced with pressure to do otherwise. This lesson is particularly relevant in today's world, where individuals are often bombarded with various influences that can sway their decisions and actions. Developing a strong sense of integrity and ethical grounding is essential in resisting negative influences and making choices that align with one's values.

The story of Jezebel and her influence over Ahab also speaks to the importance of surrounding oneself with positive influences and advisors. Leaders and individuals alike benefit from having trustworthy, ethical, and wise people around them who can provide sound advice and support. In contrast, negative influences can lead to poor decision-making and unethical behavior. Ensuring that one's inner circle is composed of individuals who uphold strong moral values can help prevent the kind of destructive influence that Jezebel had over Ahab.

Furthermore, Jezebel's actions illustrate the dangers of unchecked ambition and the lengths to which individuals will go to achieve their desires. Her relentless pursuit of power and control led her to manipulate and incite Ahab to commit grievous sins. In contemporary society, this is seen in various scenarios where individuals or groups manipulate others to fulfill their ambitions, often at the expense of ethical considerations and the well-being of others. The pursuit of power, wealth, or status without regard for morality can lead to significant harm, both to those directly involved and to the broader community.

The parallels between Jezebel's behavior and modern-day scenarios also highlight the need for accountability and transparency in all areas of life. When individuals or leaders are not held accountable for their actions, the likelihood of unethical behavior increases. Systems of accountability, whether through legal frameworks, organizational policies, or social norms, are essential in curbing the negative influence of those who seek to stir others to do wrong. Promoting transparency and accountability helps to ensure that those in positions of influence are held responsible for their actions and that ethical behavior is upheld.

In conclusion, Jezebel's behavior as described in 1 Kings 21:25, where she stirred Ahab to commit wickedness, provides a powerful example of the dangers of negative influence and the importance of ethical leadership and personal integrity. Her actions led Ahab to abandon his moral principles and engage in deeply offensive deeds, highlighting the destructive power of manipulative and malevolent influence. The parallels to modern-day scenarios in politics, business, and personal contexts underscore the enduring relevance of this story and the importance of promoting ethical behavior, accountability, and integrity. By reflecting on Jezebel's actions and their consequences, we can better understand the need to resist negative influences, surround ourselves with positive role models, and uphold strong moral values in all areas of life. The lessons from Jezebel's story serve as a timeless reminder of the importance of acting with integrity and the responsibility that comes with holding influence over others. Whether in ancient times or today, the need to recognize and address manipulative and unethical behaviors, and to protect individuals from exploitation and injustice, remains as crucial as ever. The ongoing struggle for justice, integrity, and ethical leadership is vital for building a just and compassionate society, where the rights and dignity of all individuals are respected and upheld. By promoting transparency, accountability, and moral courage, we can work towards a world where ethical behavior is the norm, and the destructive impact of manipulation and deceit is minimized. This story reminds us that the fight against injustice and the promotion of ethical leadership are ongoing efforts that require the commitment and vigilance of everyone in society.

Chapter 13 – The Smiting

2 Kings 9:7 And thou shalt smite the house of Ahab thy master, that I may avenge the blood of my servants the prophets, and the blood of all the servants of the LORD, at the hand of Jezebel.

In 2 Kings 9:7, the Bible reveals a momentous decree about Jezebel's fate: "And you shall strike down the house of Ahab your master, so that I may avenge on Jezebel the blood of my servants the prophets, and the blood of all the servants of the Lord." This verse underscores the divine retribution decreed against Jezebel, signifying a judgment for her numerous atrocities, particularly her role in orchestrating the murder of God's prophets and other servants. Jezebel's behavior was marked by relentless cruelty, manipulation, and a fierce determination to eradicate those who stood in opposition to her and her husband Ahab's reign. Her actions brought about not only widespread idolatry and corruption but also a reign of terror where dissent was met with ruthless violence. This divine mandate to "smite" the house of Ahab, and specifically Jezebel, highlights the inevitable consequences of her wickedness and the justice that was to be meted out for her heinous acts.

Comparing Jezebel's behavior and the concept of "smiting" her for her crimes to modern-day scenarios, we can see many parallels where individuals in power use their influence to commit atrocities, only to eventually face retribution. In contemporary society, leaders or influential figures who engage in corruption, human rights abuses, and other forms of injustice often face consequences, whether through legal systems, revolutions, or other forms of accountability. For instance, political leaders who misuse their power to suppress opposition, commit atrocities, or engage in large-scale corruption are sometimes deposed, tried, and punished by national or international courts. Examples include former leaders who have faced trials for war crimes, genocide, or crimes against humanity. These modern instances reflect the biblical principle of divine justice, where those who commit great wrongs are eventually held accountable for their actions.

In the corporate world, executives or business leaders who engage in unethical practices, such as fraud, exploitation, or environmental destruction, often face severe consequences as well. Legal actions, fines, and imprisonment are some of the repercussions that can befall those who prioritize personal gain over ethical conduct. Companies involved in massive scandals, such as those related to financial fraud or environmental disasters, see their reputations tarnished and their leaders held responsible. This modern equivalent of "smiting" ensures that justice is served and serves as a deterrent to others who might consider engaging in similar unethical behavior.

On a societal level, individuals who perpetrate violence, discrimination, or other forms of injustice against vulnerable populations often face social and legal consequences. Movements for justice and equality work tirelessly to expose and combat such behaviors, ensuring that perpetrators are brought to justice. For example, perpetrators of hate crimes or systemic discrimination are increasingly being held accountable through legal systems and public condemnation. Social justice movements play a crucial role in highlighting injustices and mobilizing collective action to "smite" those who harm others through their prejudiced and violent actions.

Moreover, Jezebel's story emphasizes the importance of moral integrity and the consequences of abandoning ethical principles. Her relentless pursuit of power through manipulation, violence, and corruption led to her downfall and the eventual smiting of her house. This serves as a stark reminder that actions driven by unethical motives and disregard for justice ultimately lead to destruction and retribution. In modern contexts, this principle underscores the importance of ethical leadership and personal integrity. Leaders and individuals who uphold ethical standards, even in the face of adversity, contribute to a more just and equitable society, whereas those who deviate from these principles risk significant consequences.

Jezebel's fate also highlights the role of divine or moral justice as a fundamental aspect of human society. Many cultures and religions believe in some form of ultimate justice, where individuals are held accountable for their actions by a higher power or moral law. This belief in justice serves as a guiding principle for behavior, encouraging individuals to act ethically and consider the long-term consequences of their actions. The concept of divine retribution, as seen in Jezebel's story, reinforces the idea that justice is an inevitable outcome for those who commit grievous wrongs.

The story of Jezebel and the mandate to smite her and her house also illustrate the dangers of unchecked power and the importance of accountability mechanisms. When individuals in positions of power are not held accountable, they can engage in increasingly destructive behaviors, as Jezebel did. Modern systems of governance emphasize the need for checks and balances, transparency, and accountability to prevent the abuse of power. Ensuring that leaders are held accountable through democratic processes, legal frameworks, and public scrutiny is crucial in maintaining a just and fair society.

Furthermore, the biblical narrative of smiting Jezebel can be seen as a metaphor for the broader struggle against evil and injustice. It symbolizes the collective effort required to confront and eliminate harmful influences and behaviors within society. This struggle is ongoing in modern times, as individuals and groups work to address various forms of injustice, from systemic racism and corruption to environmental degradation and human rights abuses. The fight against such injustices requires vigilance, determination, and a commitment to ethical principles, much like the divine mandate to bring justice to Jezebel and her house.

Jezebel's story also serves as a reminder of the potential for redemption and the importance of seeking forgiveness and making amends. While Jezebel herself did not seek redemption, her fate illustrates the consequences of failing to do so. In modern contexts, individuals and leaders who acknowledge their wrongdoings and take steps to make amends can often find a path to redemption and reconciliation. This process of seeking forgiveness and making restitution is essential in healing and restoring justice within communities.

In conclusion, Jezebel's behavior as described in 2 Kings 9:7, where she faces the divine decree to be smitten for her atrocities, provides a powerful example of the inevitable consequences of unethical behavior and the abuse of power. Her actions led to widespread suffering and corruption, ultimately resulting in divine retribution. The parallels to modern-day scenarios in politics, business, and social contexts underscore the enduring relevance of this story and the importance of ethical leadership, accountability, and justice. By reflecting on Jezebel's actions and their consequences, we can better understand the need to promote integrity, moral courage, and justice in all areas of life. The lessons from Jezebel's story serve as a timeless reminder of the importance of acting with integrity and the responsibility that comes with holding influence over others. Whether in ancient times or today, the need to recognize and address manipulative and unethical behaviors, and to protect individuals from exploitation and injustice, remains as crucial as ever. The ongoing struggle for justice, integrity, and ethical leadership is vital for building a just and compassionate society, where the rights and dignity of all individuals are respected and upheld. By promoting transparency, accountability, and moral courage, we can work towards a world where ethical behavior is the norm, and the destructive impact of manipulation and deceit is minimized. This story reminds us that the fight against injustice and the promotion of ethical leadership are ongoing efforts that require the commitment and vigilance of everyone in society.

Chapter 14 – Shamed

2 Kings 9:10 And the dogs shall eat Jezebel in the portion of Jezreel, and there shall be none to bury her. And he opened the door, and fled.

In 2 Kings 9:10, the Bible portrays a dramatic and powerful moment where the prophet Elijah declares Jezebel's fate: "And the dogs shall eat Jezebel in the territory of Jezreel, and none shall bury her." This verse underscores the severe divine judgment and shame that would befall Jezebel as a result of her numerous evil deeds, including her manipulation, idolatry, and ruthless murders. The prophecy of Jezebel being eaten by dogs and left unburied represents the ultimate disgrace and dishonor in ancient times, where burial was a sacred act and being left unburied was considered a fate worse than death. Jezebel's actions, which included leading Israel into idolatry, orchestrating the murder of Naboth, and killing prophets of the Lord, culminated in this ignominious end. Her shameful demise serves as a powerful reminder of the consequences of a life led by wickedness and the inevitable downfall that follows such a path. This biblical account of Jezebel's shaming has striking parallels to modern-day scenarios where individuals in positions of power or influence engage in unethical or criminal behavior, ultimately facing public disgrace and the destruction of their legacies.

In today's world, we often witness similar situations where powerful figures, whether in politics, business, or entertainment, fall from grace due to their unethical actions. The concept of being "shamed" in the modern era can take various forms, including public scandals, legal repercussions, and social ostracism. Just as Jezebel was shamed for her misdeeds, contemporary leaders and celebrities who engage in corruption, abuse, or other immoral activities often face intense public scrutiny and condemnation. Media coverage, social media platforms, and investigative journalism play crucial roles in exposing these wrongdoings, leading to a loss of reputation, credibility, and, in some cases, personal freedom.

In politics, leaders who abuse their power, engage in corruption, or violate the trust of their constituents often find themselves shamed and disgraced. Scandals involving embezzlement, abuse of power, and other forms of corruption frequently lead to investigations, trials, and, if found guilty, imprisonment. These political figures, once held in high regard, face public humiliation and the collapse of their careers. The fall of such leaders mirrors the disgrace Jezebel experienced, serving as a reminder that those who misuse their power and act unethically will ultimately be held accountable and shamed for their actions.

In the corporate world, executives and business leaders who engage in fraudulent activities, exploit workers, or engage in other unethical practices can also face severe repercussions. Whistleblowers, investigative journalists, and regulatory bodies often expose these malpractices, leading to public outrage, legal actions, and significant financial and reputational damage. Companies involved in major scandals, such as environmental disasters or financial fraud, see their leaders shamed and their businesses suffer long-term consequences. The public shaming of these corporate leaders serves as a powerful deterrent, emphasizing the importance of ethical conduct and accountability in the business world.

In the entertainment industry, celebrities and public figures who engage in criminal or immoral behavior often experience public shaming and career downfall. Allegations of sexual misconduct, substance abuse, or other forms of inappropriate behavior can quickly lead to a loss of endorsements, contracts, and public support. The #MeToo movement, for example, has brought to light numerous cases of sexual harassment and assault, leading to the shaming and downfall of many high-profile individuals. These public figures, like Jezebel, face the harsh reality that their actions have consequences, and their legacies are permanently tarnished by their misdeeds.

On a personal level, individuals who engage in unethical behavior in their relationships, workplaces, or communities may also face shame and ostracism. Acts of betrayal, dishonesty, or exploitation can lead to damaged relationships, loss of trust, and social isolation. The concept of being "shamed" extends beyond public figures to everyday individuals who must confront the consequences of their actions. The shaming of Jezebel for her evil deeds resonates with the experiences of those who face the repercussions of their unethical behavior, highlighting the universal principle that actions driven by malice or self-interest ultimately lead to disgrace and dishonor.

Furthermore, Jezebel's story underscores the broader theme of justice and the inevitable exposure of wrongdoing. In modern society, the mechanisms for exposing and addressing unethical behavior have become more sophisticated and pervasive. Investigative journalism, social media, and legal systems play crucial roles in uncovering and addressing misconduct. The public shaming of individuals who engage in wrongdoing serves as a form of societal justice, ensuring that those who harm others are held accountable. This process of exposing and shaming wrongdoers reinforces the importance of transparency, accountability, and ethical behavior in all aspects of life.

Jezebel's fate also highlights the importance of moral integrity and the long-term consequences of abandoning ethical principles. Her relentless pursuit of power through manipulation, deceit, and violence led to her ultimate disgrace and shaming. This serves as a cautionary tale for individuals in positions of power and influence, emphasizing the need to uphold moral values and ethical standards. In contemporary society, leaders and individuals who prioritize integrity and ethical behavior are more likely to build lasting legacies and earn the respect and trust of those around them.

The parallels between Jezebel's shaming and modern-day scenarios also emphasize the role of community and collective action in addressing wrongdoing. Just as the prophecy of Jezebel's fate was fulfilled through the actions of others, modern society relies on collective efforts to hold wrongdoers accountable. Advocacy groups, activists, and concerned citizens play essential roles in exposing and addressing unethical behavior, ensuring that justice is served. These collective efforts help to create a more just and equitable society, where individuals are encouraged to act ethically and are held accountable for their actions.

Moreover, Jezebel's story serves as a reminder of the potential for redemption and the importance of seeking forgiveness and making amends. While Jezebel herself did not seek redemption, her fate illustrates the consequences of failing to do so. In modern contexts, individuals who acknowledge their wrongdoings and take steps to make amends can often find a path to redemption and reconciliation. This process of seeking forgiveness and making restitution is essential in healing and restoring justice within communities.

In conclusion, Jezebel's behavior as described in 2 Kings 9:10, where she faces a divine sentence of being eaten by dogs and left unburied, represents the ultimate shame and dishonor for her wicked deeds. Her actions, driven by manipulation, idolatry, and ruthless violence, led to her disgraceful end, serving as a powerful reminder of the consequences of a life led by unethical behavior. The parallels to modern-day scenarios in politics, business, entertainment, and personal contexts underscore the enduring relevance of this story and the importance of ethical conduct, accountability, and justice. By reflecting on Jezebel's actions and their consequences, we can better understand the need to promote integrity, moral courage, and justice in all areas of life. The lessons from Jezebel's story serve as a timeless reminder of the importance of acting with integrity and the responsibility that comes with holding influence over others. Whether in ancient times or today, the need to recognize and address manipulative and unethical behaviors, and to protect individuals from exploitation and injustice, remains as crucial as ever. The ongoing struggle for justice, integrity, and ethical leadership is vital for building a just and compassionate society, where the rights and dignity of all individuals are respected and upheld. By promoting transparency, accountability, and moral courage, we can work towards a world where ethical behavior is the norm, and the destructive impact of manipulation and deceit is minimized. This story reminds us that the fight against injustice and the promotion of ethical leadership are ongoing efforts that require the commitment and vigilance of everyone in society. Jezebel's shaming, both in her time and as a metaphor for modern consequences, underscores the universal principle that wrongdoing will eventually be exposed and addressed, reinforcing the enduring value of justice and ethical conduct in building a better world.

Chapter 15 – Sorceries

2 Kings 9:22 And it came to pass, when Joram saw Jehu, that he said, Is it peace, Jehu? And he answered, What peace, so long as the whoredoms of thy mother Jezebel and her witchcrafts are so many?

In 2 Kings 9:22, the Bible presents a dramatic confrontation between Jehu and Joram, where Joram asks, "Is it peace, Jehu?" to which Jehu responds, "What peace, so long as the harlotries of your mother Jezebel and her sorceries are so many?" This verse highlights the wickedness of Jezebel, emphasizing her involvement in sorceries and idolatrous practices, which were considered abhorrent and destructive. Jezebel's use of sorceries and harlotries refers to her deep engagement in occult practices and her role in leading Israel into idolatry, turning them away from worshipping the true God. These actions were not only spiritual betrayals but also acts that corrupted and destabilized the social and moral fabric of the nation. Jezebel's influence through these dark practices exemplifies how individuals in power can use their influence to lead others astray, promoting practices that are harmful and morally corrupt. This depiction of Jezebel and her sorceries can be compared to modern-day behaviors where people in influential positions use manipulative, deceptive, or corrupt practices to control others and achieve their goals.

In today's world, similar behaviors can be observed in various contexts, from political corruption to manipulative leadership in different sectors. In politics, some leaders use propaganda, lies, and manipulation to maintain control and influence over the population. Just as Jezebel used her sorceries to lead people away from their faith and into idolatry, modern politicians might exploit people's fears and prejudices, spreading misinformation to secure their power. This manipulation undermines the integrity of democratic institutions and erodes public trust, creating a toxic environment where truth and justice are overshadowed by deceit and self-interest. The use of state machinery to disseminate false information and suppress opposition can be seen as a contemporary parallel to the sorceries of Jezebel, where the truth is distorted, and people's perceptions are manipulated to serve the interests of those in power.

In the corporate world, leaders may engage in unethical practices to gain a competitive edge, much like Jezebel's sorceries. This can include fraudulent activities, exploiting loopholes, or manipulating market conditions to benefit their companies while harming competitors and consumers. These actions, driven by greed and the desire for power, mirror Jezebel's use of sorcery and manipulation to achieve her ends. The consequences of such corporate sorceries can be far-reaching, leading to financial crises, loss of jobs, and economic instability, much like the social and moral decay brought about by Jezebel's actions.

On a personal level, individuals who engage in manipulative or deceitful behaviors to control or harm others reflect Jezebel's use of sorceries. This can be seen in toxic relationships where one person uses emotional manipulation, lies, and deceit to dominate and control their partner. Such behaviors can cause significant psychological harm and undermine the victim's sense of self-worth and autonomy. In communities, individuals who spread rumors or engage in gossip to manipulate social dynamics and harm others' reputations are also engaging in modern-day sorceries, using deceit and manipulation to wield power over others.

Jezebel's actions also highlight the broader theme of the dangers of occult practices and the allure of power through dark means. Throughout history, individuals and groups have turned to occult practices, believing they can gain control over others or secure their desires through supernatural means. While modern society may not always recognize these practices as "sorceries," the underlying principle of using unethical means to achieve power and control remains relevant. The pursuit of power through any means necessary, including harmful and deceitful practices, is a recurring issue in human behavior.

Moreover, Jezebel's story serves as a cautionary tale about the consequences of abandoning ethical principles in favor of power and control. Her engagement in sorceries and the subsequent moral and social decay it caused in Israel is a stark reminder of the destructive potential of such behavior. In contemporary society, this lesson underscores the importance of maintaining ethical standards and integrity, whether in leadership, business, or personal relationships. The pursuit of power without regard for ethics and morality can lead to widespread harm and destabilization, as seen in the story of Jezebel.

The parallels between Jezebel's sorceries and modern-day manipulative practices also emphasize the need for vigilance and ethical leadership. Leaders who prioritize transparency, accountability, and truth can help prevent the kind of corruption and moral decay that Jezebel's actions brought about. Encouraging a culture of integrity and ethical behavior is crucial in countering the manipulative and deceitful practices that can erode trust and harm society.

Jezebel's story also underscores the role of spiritual and moral guidance in maintaining a just and stable society. Her turn to sorceries and idolatry led Israel away from their faith and ethical principles, causing significant moral and social disruption. In modern times, the importance of upholding spiritual and moral values is evident in the efforts of various religious and ethical leaders who work to promote justice, compassion, and integrity. These leaders play a crucial role in countering the negative influences of those who seek power through unethical means, much like the prophets who stood against Jezebel's idolatry and sorceries.

Furthermore, the story of Jezebel and her sorceries illustrates the power of influence and the responsibility that comes with it. Jezebel used her position to lead others into practices that were harmful and destructive, highlighting how influential individuals can shape the behavior and beliefs of those around them. In contemporary society, this principle is evident in the influence wielded by politicians, business leaders, celebrities, and social media personalities. The actions and words of these individuals can have significant impacts on public opinion, social norms, and ethical standards. It is essential for those in positions of influence to use their power responsibly and ethically, promoting behaviors and practices that contribute to the common good rather than personal gain.

The story of Jezebel and her eventual downfall also serves as a reminder of the ultimate consequences of unethical behavior. Despite her initial success in using sorceries to manipulate and control, Jezebel's actions led to her disgrace and death. This outcome underscores the idea that unethical practices, while they may provide short-term gains, ultimately lead to negative consequences. In modern contexts, this principle can be seen in the eventual exposure and downfall of corrupt leaders, unethical business practices, and manipulative individuals. The long-term consequences of unethical behavior often include loss of trust, legal repercussions, and social ostracism, reinforcing the importance of maintaining ethical integrity.

In conclusion, Jezebel's behavior as described in 2 Kings 9:22, where her sorceries and harlotries are cited as reasons for the lack of peace in Israel, provides a powerful example of the destructive impact of manipulative and unethical practices. Her actions led to significant moral and social decay, ultimately resulting in her downfall and disgrace. The parallels to modern-day scenarios in politics, business, and personal relationships underscore the enduring relevance of this story and the importance of ethical conduct, accountability, and integrity. By reflecting on Jezebel's actions and their consequences, we can better understand the need to promote ethical behavior and resist the allure of power through unethical means. The lessons from Jezebel's story serve as a timeless reminder of the importance of acting with integrity and the responsibility that comes with holding influence over others. Whether in ancient times or today, the need to recognize and address manipulative and unethical behaviors, and to protect individuals from exploitation and injustice, remains as crucial as ever. The ongoing struggle for justice, integrity, and ethical leadership is vital for building a just and compassionate society, where the rights and dignity of all individuals are respected and upheld. By promoting transparency, accountability, and moral courage, we can work towards a world where ethical behavior is the norm, and the destructive impact of manipulation and deceit is minimized. This story reminds us that the fight against injustice and the promotion of ethical leadership are ongoing efforts that require the commitment and vigilance of everyone in society. Jezebel's use of sorceries and the resulting consequences serve as a powerful metaphor for the dangers of unethical practices and the ultimate triumph of justice and integrity over manipulation and deceit.

Chapter 16 – Sight

2 Kings 9:30 And when Jehu was come to Jezreel, Jezebel heard of it; and she painted her face, and tired her head, and looked out at a window.

In 2 Kings 9:30, Jezebel's behavior and her ultimate fate come sharply into focus as the Bible describes her final act of defiance. The verse states, "And when Jehu was come to Jezreel, Jezebel heard of it; and she painted her face, and tired her head, and looked out at a window." This verse depicts Jezebel using her sight and appearance in an attempt to confront Jehu, who was anointed by God to bring judgment upon her. By painting her face and adorning her head, Jezebel tried to present herself with dignity and control, possibly in an effort to seduce or intimidate Jehu, but also to maintain her regal image to the very end. This scene highlights her vanity and pride, as she relied on her outward appearance to assert her power and influence, even as she faced imminent doom. Jezebel's reliance on her sight and the manipulation of her appearance to maintain power can be compared to modern-day behaviors where individuals use their looks, image, and public persona to influence and control others.

In today's world, similar behaviors can be observed in various contexts, including politics, entertainment, and social media. Public figures often use their appearance and carefully crafted images to sway public opinion, gain support, and maintain their influence. Politicians, for example, frequently rely on their image and media presence to connect with voters, often employing makeup artists, stylists, and public relations experts to enhance their appeal. Just as Jezebel painted her face to confront Jehu, modern politicians may use their appearance and charisma to project strength and confidence, even in the face of scandal or declining popularity. This reliance on appearance can sometimes mask underlying issues or unethical behaviors, creating a disconnect between public perception and reality.

In the entertainment industry, celebrities and influencers heavily invest in their appearance and public image to attract and retain their audience. The use of makeup, fashion, and social media filters helps them maintain a certain persona that resonates with fans. Like Jezebel, who used her sight and appearance to confront Jehu, these public figures often use their looks to gain followers, endorsements, and media attention. However, this focus on appearance can sometimes lead to superficiality and a lack of authenticity, as the pressure to maintain a perfect image can overshadow genuine talent and character. The constant emphasis on physical appearance can also contribute to unrealistic beauty standards and self-esteem issues among their audience, particularly young people who may feel pressured to conform to these ideals.

On social media, individuals often curate their profiles to present the best possible version of themselves, using photos, filters, and carefully crafted posts to shape how they are perceived by others. This digital form of painting one's face, much like Jezebel did, allows people to control their image and influence their social circles. However, this can lead to a culture of comparison and competition, where people feel the need to constantly enhance their appearance and lifestyle to keep up with others. The pressure to maintain a perfect online persona can lead to anxiety, depression, and a sense of inadequacy, as the curated images rarely reflect the complexities and imperfections of real life.

Moreover, Jezebel's behavior highlights the broader theme of vanity and the reliance on superficial means to maintain power and influence. Her attempt to use her appearance to confront Jehu reflects a deeper insecurity and desperation to cling to her authority. In contemporary society, this theme is evident in the way some individuals prioritize their external image over substantive qualities such as integrity, kindness, and competence. The obsession with appearance and the superficial aspects of one's persona can detract from the importance of inner character and ethical behavior. This emphasis on looks and image can also perpetuate a culture where success is measured by outward appearances rather than genuine achievements and contributions.

Jezebel's final act of painting her face and looking out the window as Jehu approached also symbolizes the illusion of control and the facade of power. Despite her efforts to present herself as composed and powerful, her fate was already sealed by her previous actions and the divine judgment pronounced against her. This scene serves as a powerful reminder that outward appearances and superficial efforts to maintain control cannot ultimately change the reality of one's actions and their consequences. In modern contexts, this lesson underscores the importance of authenticity and the limitations of relying solely on appearance to navigate life's challenges. True power and influence come from integrity, ethical behavior, and genuine connections with others, rather than from the manipulation of one's image.

The story of Jezebel and her reliance on sight and appearance also speaks to the role of media and visual culture in shaping public perception. The proliferation of visual media, including television, film, advertising, and social media, has amplified the importance of appearance and image in contemporary society. The way individuals and public figures are portrayed visually can significantly influence public opinion and societal norms. This visual culture can perpetuate certain stereotypes and ideals, often prioritizing beauty, youth, and charisma over more substantive qualities. Just as Jezebel used her appearance to assert her power, modern media often uses visual imagery to shape narratives and influence behavior, highlighting the need for media literacy and critical thinking in navigating these influences.

Furthermore, Jezebel's story illustrates the potential pitfalls of relying on appearance and image to achieve one's goals. Her ultimate downfall, despite her efforts to maintain her regal image, serves as a cautionary tale about the fleeting nature of superficial power. In contemporary society, individuals who focus excessively on their appearance and image at the expense of ethical behavior and genuine connections may find themselves facing similar consequences. The pursuit of superficial validation can lead to a lack of fulfillment and authenticity, as well as potential public backlash and loss of credibility when the facade is inevitably exposed.

The parallels between Jezebel's behavior and modern-day reliance on appearance also emphasize the importance of promoting values such as integrity, authenticity, and substance over superficiality. Encouraging individuals, especially young people, to value inner qualities and ethical behavior can help counter the negative effects of a culture that prioritizes appearance. By fostering environments where people are appreciated for their character and contributions rather than their looks, we can build a more just and compassionate society.

In conclusion, Jezebel's behavior as described in 2 Kings 9:30, where she uses her sight and appearance to confront Jehu, provides a powerful example of the reliance on superficial means to maintain power and influence. Her actions highlight the themes of vanity, the illusion of control, and the limitations of relying on appearance to navigate life's challenges. The parallels to modern-day scenarios in politics, entertainment, social media, and personal relationships underscore the enduring relevance of this story and the importance of authenticity, integrity, and ethical behavior. By reflecting on Jezebel's actions and their consequences, we can better understand the need to promote values that prioritize inner qualities and genuine connections over superficial appearances. The lessons from Jezebel's story serve as a timeless reminder of the importance of acting with integrity and the limitations of relying solely on appearance to achieve one's goals.

Whether in ancient times or today, the need to recognize and address the superficial aspects of our culture, and to protect individuals from the pressures of maintaining a perfect image, remains as crucial as ever. The ongoing struggle for authenticity, integrity, and ethical leadership is vital for building a just and compassionate society, where the rights and dignity of all individuals are respected and upheld. By promoting transparency, accountability, and moral courage, we can work towards a world where ethical behavior is the norm, and the destructive impact of superficiality and deceit is minimized. This story reminds us that the fight against superficiality and the promotion of genuine values are ongoing efforts that require the commitment and vigilance of everyone in society. Jezebel's use of sight and appearance, and the resulting consequences, serve as a powerful metaphor for the dangers of relying on superficial means and the ultimate triumph of authenticity and integrity over manipulation and deceit.

Chapter 17 – Statement

2 Kings 9:36 Wherefore they came again, and told him. And he said, This is the word of the LORD, which he spake by his servant Elijah the Tishbite, saying, In the portion of Jezreel shall dogs eat the flesh of Jezebel:

In 2 Kings 9:36, the Bible recounts a grim and significant moment, where Jehu's men return to him and say, "This is the word of the Lord that he spoke by his servant Elijah the Tishbite: 'In the territory of Jezreel the dogs shall eat the flesh of Jezebel.'" This statement fulfills the prophecy given by Elijah as a divine judgment against Jezebel for her many sins, including idolatry, murder, and leading Israel into wickedness. This declaration underscores the severity of Jezebel's crimes and the ultimate divine retribution she faced, serving as a powerful testament to the belief that justice, no matter how delayed, will prevail. Jezebel's fate, as proclaimed in this statement, illustrates the ultimate consequences of a life marked by manipulation, cruelty, and defiance against God's commandments. Her story, culminating in this fulfillment of prophecy, highlights the inevitable downfall that accompanies such a path of wickedness. This biblical account can be compared to modern-day scenarios where individuals or leaders who engage in unethical, harmful, or illegal actions eventually face the consequences of their behavior, often through legal systems, public exposure, or other forms of accountability.

In today's world, the idea that justice will ultimately be served resonates deeply, especially in the context of powerful individuals or leaders who believe they are untouchable due to their influence or resources. Similar to how Jezebel believed she could act with impunity, many contemporary figures engage in corruption, abuse of power, and other immoral activities, thinking they can evade accountability. However, history and current events show that such individuals often face repercussions, whether through legal action, public scandal, or other forms of societal judgment. This modern parallel to Jezebel's story underscores the importance of accountability and the principle that no one is above the law.

In politics, numerous leaders have fallen from grace after being exposed for their corrupt practices, human rights abuses, or other unethical behaviors. Just as Jezebel faced divine judgment, modern politicians often face the court of public opinion, legal systems, and international bodies that hold them accountable for their actions. For instance, leaders involved in embezzlement, electoral fraud, or crimes against humanity frequently face trials, imprisonment, and a loss of reputation. The public and international community's role in demanding justice and transparency mirrors the prophetic fulfillment seen in Jezebel's story, reinforcing the notion that justice, while sometimes delayed, is inevitable.

In the corporate sector, executives who engage in fraudulent activities, exploit workers, or violate environmental regulations often face severe consequences as well. Whistleblowers, investigative journalists, and regulatory agencies play crucial roles in uncovering these malpractices, leading to legal actions, financial penalties, and reputational damage. These outcomes highlight how modern mechanisms for ensuring accountability and justice operate, much like the divine prophecy fulfilled against Jezebel. The exposure and punishment of corporate wrongdoing serve as a deterrent and a reminder that unethical behavior will eventually be confronted and penalized.

On a personal level, individuals who engage in deceitful, harmful, or illegal actions also experience the consequences of their behavior. This can manifest in various ways, such as legal repercussions, social ostracism, and damaged relationships. The statement about Jezebel's fate serves as a metaphor for the broader principle that actions driven by malice, greed, or defiance of moral laws ultimately lead to negative outcomes. In contemporary society, this is seen in cases where individuals face justice for crimes, dishonesty, or betrayal, reinforcing the importance of ethical conduct and personal integrity.

Jezebel's story also highlights the role of prophetic voices and truth-tellers in society. Elijah's prophecy about Jezebel's fate was a bold declaration of truth against a powerful and wicked figure. In modern times, whistleblowers, journalists, activists, and other truth-tellers play a similar role by exposing wrongdoing and advocating for justice. These individuals often face significant risks and challenges in their efforts to hold powerful figures accountable, yet their work is essential in ensuring transparency and upholding ethical standards. The fulfillment of Elijah's prophecy serves as a reminder of the importance and impact of speaking truth to power, regardless of the obstacles.

Moreover, Jezebel's fate underscores the broader theme of divine or moral justice that transcends human legal systems. Many cultures and religions uphold the belief that a higher power ensures that justice is ultimately served, even when human systems fail. This belief in divine justice provides hope and reassurance that those who commit great wrongs will face consequences, reinforcing the moral fabric of society. Jezebel's story serves as a powerful illustration of this principle, reminding us that ethical behavior and adherence to moral laws are fundamental to a just society.

The parallels between Jezebel's downfall and modern-day scenarios also emphasize the importance of ethical leadership and the need for robust systems of accountability. Leaders who prioritize integrity, transparency, and justice help build trust and stability within their organizations and communities. Conversely, those who engage in corrupt or unethical practices erode trust and create environments of fear and injustice. By fostering a culture of accountability and ethical conduct, societies can prevent the kind of moral decay and corruption exemplified by Jezebel's reign.

In the context of social movements and activism, Jezebel's story and the fulfillment of Elijah's prophecy highlight the power of collective action in demanding justice. Activists and social movements often work tirelessly to expose injustices and hold perpetrators accountable, much like Elijah's prophetic declaration aimed to bring about divine justice. These movements play a crucial role in challenging systemic corruption and advocating for the rights and dignity of all individuals. The perseverance and determination of activists in the face of adversity reflect the enduring struggle for justice and the belief that truth and righteousness will ultimately prevail.

Furthermore, Jezebel's ultimate fate serves as a reminder of the potential for redemption and the importance of seeking forgiveness and making amends. While Jezebel did not seek redemption, her story illustrates the severe consequences of failing to do so. In modern contexts, individuals and leaders who acknowledge their wrongdoings and take steps to make amends can often find a path to redemption and reconciliation. This process of seeking forgiveness and making restitution is essential in healing and restoring justice within communities.

In conclusion, Jezebel's behavior as described in 2 Kings 9:36, where her fate is confirmed by the fulfillment of Elijah's prophecy, provides a powerful example of the consequences of a life marked by unethical and harmful actions. Her story, culminating in her shameful end, serves as a testament to the principle that justice will ultimately be served. The parallels to modern-day scenarios in politics, business, and personal contexts underscore the enduring relevance of this story and the importance of accountability, ethical conduct, and integrity. By reflecting on Jezebel's actions and their consequences, we can better understand the need to promote justice, transparency, and moral courage in all areas of life. The lessons from Jezebel's story serve as a timeless reminder of the importance of acting with integrity and the responsibility that comes with holding influence over others. Whether in ancient times or today, the need to recognize and address unethical behaviors, and to protect individuals from exploitation and injustice, remains as crucial as ever. The ongoing struggle for justice, integrity, and ethical leadership is vital for building a just and compassionate society, where the rights and dignity of all individuals are respected and upheld. By promoting transparency, accountability, and moral courage, we can work towards a world where ethical behavior is the norm, and the destructive impact of manipulation and deceit is minimized. This story reminds us that the fight against injustice and the promotion of ethical leadership are ongoing efforts that require the commitment and vigilance of everyone in society. Jezebel's ultimate fate, as foretold by Elijah and realized in her death, underscores the universal principle that wrongdoing will eventually be exposed and addressed, reinforcing the enduring value of justice and ethical conduct in building a better world.

Chapter 18 – Scorned

2 Kings 9:37 And the carcase of Jezebel shall be as dung upon the face of the field in the portion of Jezreel; so that they shall not say, This is Jezebel.

In 2 Kings 9:37, the Bible describes the final and gruesome end of Jezebel with the verse, "And the carcass of Jezebel shall be as dung upon the face of the field in the portion of Jezreel, so that they shall not say, This is Jezebel." This verse signifies the ultimate scorn and disgrace that Jezebel faced as a consequence of her evil deeds. Her body, left unburied and desecrated, symbolized the utter contempt and rejection by both divine judgment and society. Jezebel's behavior, characterized by manipulation, idolatry, murder, and incitement to sin, led to her being scorned and humiliated in death. Her fate was a stark message about the inevitable downfall that comes from a life of wickedness and tyranny. This depiction of Jezebel's end serves as a powerful reminder that no matter how powerful or influential one might be, unethical and immoral actions will eventually lead to severe repercussions and societal scorn. This biblical account can be compared to modern-day scenarios where individuals or leaders engage in corrupt, unethical, or criminal behaviors, eventually facing public disgrace, rejection, and condemnation.

In today's world, similar behaviors and their consequences can be observed across various sectors, including politics, business, entertainment, and social media. Public figures who abuse their power, engage in corruption, or commit crimes often find themselves scorned by society once their actions come to light. This public scorn is manifested through legal repercussions, media scrutiny, loss of reputation, and social ostracism. Just as Jezebel's body was left to be eaten by dogs, symbolizing the complete rejection by society, modern-day figures who fall from grace often experience a metaphorical equivalent, where they are cast out from their positions of power and influence, their legacies tarnished by their actions.

In the political arena, leaders who engage in corruption, abuse of power, or human rights violations often face public scorn and legal consequences. Scandals involving embezzlement, electoral fraud, or oppression typically lead to investigations, trials, and, if found guilty, imprisonment. These leaders, once held in high esteem, find themselves rejected and despised by the public and their peers. The fall of such leaders serves as a potent reminder of the importance of integrity and accountability in governance. Public scorn and the resulting consequences act as a deterrent to others who might consider engaging in similar behaviors, reinforcing the principle that no one is above the law.

In the corporate world, executives and business leaders who engage in fraudulent activities, exploit workers, or violate environmental laws often face severe backlash from the public, investors, and regulatory bodies. Whistleblowers, investigative journalists, and watchdog organizations play crucial roles in exposing these unethical practices, leading to legal actions, financial penalties, and significant damage to the company's reputation. The public scorn directed at these corporate leaders mirrors the biblical scorn faced by Jezebel, highlighting the societal demand for ethical business practices and corporate responsibility. The exposure and condemnation of corporate malfeasance serve as a reminder that the pursuit of profit must be balanced with ethical considerations and respect for the law.

In the entertainment industry, celebrities and public figures who engage in criminal or immoral behavior often experience public scorn and career downfall. Allegations of sexual misconduct, substance abuse, or other forms of inappropriate behavior can quickly lead to a loss of endorsements, contracts, and public support. Movements such as #MeToo have brought to light numerous cases of harassment and abuse, leading to the shaming and downfall of many high-profile individuals. These public figures, much like Jezebel, face the harsh reality that their actions have consequences, and their legacies are permanently marred by their misdeeds. The public scorn they face underscores the importance of accountability and the impact of societal values on personal and professional conduct.

On social media, individuals who engage in harmful or unethical behavior can quickly become the target of widespread condemnation. Viral videos, posts, and online campaigns can bring attention to actions such as racism, bullying, or other forms of misconduct, leading to public shaming and social ostracism. The rapid spread of information on social media means that individuals can be held accountable by a global audience, facing scorn and rejection from people around the world. This modern form of public scorn serves as a powerful tool for promoting social justice and holding individuals accountable for their actions, much like the divine judgment that befell Jezebel.

Jezebel's story also highlights the importance of moral integrity and the long-term consequences of abandoning ethical principles. Her relentless pursuit of power through manipulation, deceit, and violence led to her ultimate disgrace and shaming. This serves as a cautionary tale for individuals in positions of power and influence, emphasizing the need to uphold moral values and ethical standards. In contemporary society, leaders and individuals who prioritize integrity and ethical behavior are more likely to build lasting legacies and earn the respect and trust of those around them.

The parallels between Jezebel's scorned fate and modern-day scenarios also emphasize the role of community and collective action in addressing wrongdoing. Just as the prophecy of Jezebel's fate was fulfilled through the actions of others, modern society relies on collective efforts to hold wrongdoers accountable. Advocacy groups, activists, and concerned citizens play essential roles in exposing and addressing unethical behavior, ensuring that justice is served. These collective efforts help to create a more just and equitable society, where individuals are encouraged to act ethically and are held accountable for their actions.

Moreover, Jezebel's story serves as a reminder of the potential for redemption and the importance of seeking forgiveness and making amends. While Jezebel herself did not seek redemption, her fate illustrates the severe consequences of failing to do so. In modern contexts, individuals who acknowledge their wrongdoings and take steps to make amends can often find a path to redemption and reconciliation. This process of seeking forgiveness and making restitution is essential in healing and restoring justice within communities.

In conclusion, Jezebel's behavior as described in 2 Kings 9:37, where her body is left as dung upon the field, symbolizing the ultimate scorn and rejection, provides a powerful example of the consequences of a life marked by unethical and harmful actions. Her story, culminating in her disgraceful end, serves as a testament to the principle that justice will ultimately be served, and those who engage in wickedness will face societal scorn and rejection. The parallels to modern-day scenarios in politics, business, entertainment, social media, and personal contexts underscore the enduring relevance of this story and the importance of accountability, ethical conduct, and integrity. By reflecting on Jezebel's actions and their consequences, we can better understand the need to promote justice, transparency, and moral courage in all areas of life. The lessons from Jezebel's story serve as a timeless reminder of the importance of acting with integrity and the responsibility that comes with holding influence over others. Whether in ancient times or today, the need to recognize and address unethical behaviors, and to protect individuals from exploitation and injustice, remains as crucial as ever. The ongoing struggle for justice, integrity, and ethical leadership is vital for building a just and compassionate society, where the rights and dignity of all individuals are respected and upheld. By promoting transparency, accountability, and moral courage, we can work towards a world where ethical behavior is the norm, and the destructive impact of manipulation and deceit is minimized. This story reminds us that the fight against injustice and the promotion of ethical leadership are ongoing efforts that require the commitment and vigilance of everyone in society. Jezebel's ultimate fate, being scorned and rejected, underscores the universal principle that wrongdoing will eventually be exposed and addressed, reinforcing the enduring value of justice and ethical conduct in building a better world.

Chapter 19 – Seduce

Revelation 2:20 Notwithstanding I have a few things against thee, because thou sufferest that woman Jezebel, which calleth herself a prophetess, to teach and to seduce my servants to commit fornication, and to eat things sacrificed unto idols.

In Revelation 2:20, the Bible warns about the dangers of immoral and deceptive influences, drawing a direct comparison to Jezebel's behavior. The verse says, "Nevertheless, I have this against you: You tolerate that woman Jezebel, who calls herself a prophet. By her teaching, she misleads my servants into sexual immorality and the eating of food sacrificed to idols." This passage references a figure named Jezebel, whose actions are reminiscent of the original Jezebel's manipulative and immoral behavior, seducing others into sin and idolatry. Jezebel's behavior in this context highlights her ability to seduce and corrupt, using her influence to lead people away from their faith and moral principles. Her seductive tactics were not limited to physical seduction but extended to leading others into practices that were spiritually corrupt and morally reprehensible. This biblical portrayal of Jezebel's seduction and manipulation serves as a cautionary tale about the power of deceit and the dangers of tolerating immoral influences. In today's world, we can observe similar behaviors where individuals or entities use seduction, manipulation, and deceit to lead others astray, often with devastating consequences.

In contemporary society, the concept of seduction extends beyond physical allure to include psychological manipulation and the exploitation of vulnerabilities. For instance, in the world of politics, some leaders use charismatic rhetoric and false promises to seduce the public, gaining support while hiding their true intentions. These leaders may engage in propaganda, spreading misinformation to manipulate public opinion and maintain power. Much like Jezebel, who seduced people into idolatry and immorality, these modern political figures can lead nations into division, corruption, and moral decay. The seductive power of charismatic leaders highlights the importance of critical thinking and the need for transparency and accountability in governance.

In the business sector, companies and marketers often use seductive advertising tactics to lure consumers into buying products or services, sometimes through deceptive means. These tactics can include false advertising, exaggerated claims, or the manipulation of consumer emotions and desires. By creating an illusion of necessity or desirability, businesses can lead consumers to make decisions that are not in their best interest, often prioritizing profit over ethics. This modern form of seduction mirrors Jezebel's manipulation, where the pursuit of personal gain leads to the exploitation and harm of others. The prevalence of such practices underscores the need for consumer awareness and stricter regulations to ensure ethical business conduct.

On social media, influencers and content creators often use seductive imagery and persuasive language to attract followers and promote products, lifestyles, or ideologies. This can involve creating an idealized and often unrealistic portrayal of life, leading followers to aspire to unattainable standards. The pressure to conform to these standards can result in negative self-esteem, mental health issues, and unhealthy behaviors, particularly among young people. Just as Jezebel seduced her followers into idolatry and immorality, modern social media influencers can lead their audience into superficiality, consumerism, and unrealistic expectations. The impact of social media seduction highlights the importance of promoting authentic and positive content that encourages healthy self-esteem and realistic goals.

In personal relationships, individuals can use seduction and manipulation to control or exploit their partners. This can involve emotional manipulation, gaslighting, and other tactics to gain power and maintain control over the other person. These behaviors can result in toxic and abusive relationships, causing significant emotional and psychological harm. The story of Jezebel's seduction serves as a reminder of the destructive power of manipulation in personal interactions and the importance of fostering relationships based on mutual respect, trust, and integrity.

Jezebel's behavior also underscores the broader theme of moral and spiritual seduction, where individuals or groups lead others away from ethical and spiritual principles. In various religious and spiritual contexts, false prophets and teachers can seduce followers into adopting beliefs and practices that are contrary to their faith's teachings. This can lead to spiritual confusion, division within religious communities, and a departure from foundational values. The warning against Jezebel in Revelation 2:20 highlights the need for vigilance and discernment in spiritual matters, encouraging individuals to remain steadfast in their faith and wary of deceptive influences.

The parallels between Jezebel's seductive tactics and modern-day behaviors also emphasize the importance of education and awareness in combating manipulation and deceit. By promoting critical thinking, media literacy, and ethical education, society can equip individuals with the tools to recognize and resist seductive and manipulative tactics. This involves fostering an environment where truth, integrity, and ethical behavior are valued and upheld, reducing the impact of those who seek to exploit others for personal gain.

Furthermore, Jezebel's story illustrates the potential consequences of tolerating immoral and deceptive influences. In both the biblical narrative and contemporary contexts, allowing such behaviors to persist can lead to widespread harm and moral decay. This highlights the importance of taking a proactive stance against unethical behavior, whether through personal action, community efforts, or institutional policies. By addressing and challenging immoral influences, society can work towards creating a more just and ethical environment.

The story of Jezebel and her seductive influence also serves as a reminder of the importance of personal integrity and the strength to resist temptation. Individuals are often faced with situations where they must choose between ethical principles and seductive but unethical opportunities. By cultivating strong moral values and a commitment to integrity, individuals can navigate these challenges and make decisions that align with their ethical beliefs. This personal commitment to integrity is crucial in resisting the seductive power of manipulation and deceit.

In conclusion, Jezebel's behavior as described in Revelation 2:20, where she seduces others into immorality and idolatry, provides a powerful example of the dangers of seductive and manipulative influences. Her actions led to spiritual and moral corruption, serving as a cautionary tale about the power of deceit and the importance of vigilance and integrity. The parallels to modern-day scenarios in politics, business, social media, and personal relationships underscore the enduring relevance of this story and the need for ethical conduct, critical thinking, and accountability. By reflecting on Jezebel's actions and their consequences, we can better understand the need to promote truth, integrity, and ethical behavior in all areas of life. The lessons from Jezebel's story serve as a timeless reminder of the importance of acting with integrity and the responsibility that comes with holding influence over others. Whether in ancient times or today, the need to recognize and address seductive and manipulative behaviors, and to protect individuals from exploitation and deceit, remains as crucial as ever. The ongoing struggle for justice, integrity, and ethical leadership is vital for building a just and compassionate society, where the rights and dignity of all individuals are respected and upheld. By promoting transparency, accountability, and moral courage, we can work towards a world where ethical behavior is the norm, and the destructive impact of seduction and manipulation is minimized. This story reminds us that the fight against deception and the promotion of ethical leadership are ongoing efforts that require the commitment and vigilance of everyone in society. Jezebel's seductive tactics and the resulting consequences serve as a powerful metaphor for the dangers of manipulation and the ultimate triumph of truth and integrity over deceit.

Conclusion

As we reach the conclusion of "The Jezebel Effect: Ancient Manipulations, Modern Lessons," it becomes clear that the story of Jezebel is far more than just a historical account of a wicked queen. It is a powerful allegory, deeply rooted in the verses of the King James Bible, that speaks to the timeless nature of human frailty, the corrupting influence of power, and the insidious ways in which manipulation can take hold in the hearts of individuals and societies. Through the lens of Jezebel's life and actions, we have explored how the strategies she employed—deception, coercion, and exploitation of authority—continue to manifest in various forms today, reminding us that the battle between good and evil is as relevant now as it was in the days of the Old Testament.

Jezebel's story, as recorded in 1 and 2 Kings, serves as a stark warning against the dangers of abandoning godly principles in pursuit of selfish ambition and control. Her manipulations, though successful in the short term, ultimately led to her downfall, demonstrating that the forces of darkness are always met with divine justice. This narrative highlights the importance of discernment, integrity, and unwavering faith in God, virtues that are crucial for resisting the modern-day echoes of Jezebel's spirit. The King James Bible provides us not only with a record of Jezebel's misdeeds but also with a blueprint for how to navigate the challenges posed by similar forces in our own lives.

Throughout this book, we have drawn parallels between Jezebel's ancient tactics and the manipulations we encounter today—whether in the realms of politics, business, media, or personal relationships. These modern manifestations of the Jezebel spirit often disguise themselves in subtler forms, making it all the more important for us to be vigilant and grounded in the truth of God's Word. By understanding the lessons from Jezebel's story, we are better equipped to recognize and counteract the corrosive effects of manipulation and deceit in our own lives and communities.

However, the story of Jezebel is not just a cautionary tale; it also offers a message of hope and redemption. Even in the face of great evil, God's sovereignty prevails. The downfall of Jezebel is a testament to the ultimate victory of righteousness over wickedness. For those who place their trust in God, there is assurance that, no matter how pervasive or powerful the forces of manipulation may seem, they will not stand against the truth and justice of God's kingdom. This assurance empowers us to live with courage and conviction, knowing that we are not alone in our struggles against the Jezebel spirits of our time.

In closing, "The Jezebel Effect" is a call to action for every reader. It challenges us to examine our own lives, to guard against the temptations of power and control, and to stand firm in the principles of truth and righteousness as revealed in the King James Bible. By learning from the past, we can confront the present with wisdom and courage, and build a future that honors God's will. As we move forward, let us remember the lessons of Jezebel's story, committing ourselves to live in a way that reflects the light of God's truth in a world that desperately needs it.

Don't miss out!

Visit the website below and you can sign up to receive emails whenever Joshua Rhoades publishes a new book. There's no charge and no obligation.

https://books2read.com/r/B-A-AJLBB-XEBYE

BOOKS 2 READ

Connecting independent readers to independent writers.

Did you love *The Jezebel Effect - Ancient Manipulations Modern Lessons*? Then you should read *Renewed Hope- How to Find Encouragement in God*[1] by Joshua Rhoades!

[2]

In a world where challenges and hardships seem to come at us from every side, it's easy to feel overwhelmed, discouraged, and even hopeless. We all face moments when we wonder how we will ever make it through the difficulties we encounter. But in these times, the Bible offers us a powerful example of finding strength and hope, no matter the circumstances. In 1 Samuel 30:6, we read about David, a man who faced great trials and overwhelming odds, yet in the midst of it all, "David encouraged himself in the LORD his God." This simple yet profound statement serves as the foundation for this book, "Renewed Hope- How to Find Encouragement in God." David's life was filled with ups and downs, moments of triumph and times of deep despair. He knew what it was like to be pursued by enemies, to experience loss, and to feel abandoned. Yet, even in his darkest hours, David found a way to renew his hope by turning to God. He didn't rely on his own strength or seek comfort in worldly solutions. Instead, he looked to the LORD, drawing strength and encouragement from his relationship

---

1. https://books2read.com/u/boeko1

2. https://books2read.com/u/boeko1

with God. This book is an invitation to explore how we, too, can find renewed hope and encouragement in God, just as David did. It is a guide to understanding the power of faith, prayer, and trusting in God's promises, even when life seems unbearable. Throughout these pages, we will explore practical ways to draw closer to God, to encourage ourselves in Him, and to discover the peace and strength that come from relying on the LORD. Whether you are facing a specific challenge right now or simply want to deepen your relationship with God, this book will provide you with the tools and inspiration you need to find encouragement in the LORD. As we journey together through the principles found in David's example, you will learn how to shift your focus from the problems that surround you to the God who sustains you. You will discover that no matter what life throws at you, there is always hope in the LORD, and by encouraging yourself in Him, you can face any situation with renewed strength and confidence. This is not just a book about surviving difficult times, but about thriving through them by finding your hope and encouragement in the unchanging character of God. So, whether you are struggling with personal challenges, feeling weighed down by the burdens of life, or simply seeking a deeper sense of peace and purpose, "Renewed Hope-How to Find Encouragement in God" is here to remind you that you are not alone, and that with God, there is always a reason to hope. Let David's example inspire you to turn to the LORD, to find your strength in Him, and to walk forward with a renewed sense of hope, no matter what you face.